Instructional Planning

Instructional Planning

A Guide for Teachers

Second Edition

Robert A. Reiser
and
Walter Dick

FLORIDA STATE UNIVERSITY

Allyn and Bacon
Boston • London • Toronto • Sydney • Tokyo • Singapore

Vice President, Education: Nancy Forsythe
Series Editorial Assistant: Kate Wagstaff
Manufacturing Buyer: Aloka Rathnam
Marketing Manager: Kathy Hunter
Production Administrator: Mary Beth Finch
Editorial-Production Service: Electronic Publishing Services Inc.
Cover Administrator: Suzanne Harbison

Copyright © 1996, 1989 by Allyn & Bacon
A Simon & Schuster Company
Needham Heights, Massachusetts 02194

The first edition of this book was published under the title *Planning Effective Instruction*.

Library of Congress Cataloging-in-Publication Data

Reiser, Robert A.
    Instructional planning: a guide for teachers / Robert A. Reiser and Walter Dick.—2nd ed.
        p.   cm.
    Rev. ed. of: Planning effective instruction / Walter Dick, Robert A. Reiser.
    Includes bibliographical references and index.
    ISBN 0-205-16614-8
    1. Instructional systems—United States—Design.   2. Curriculum planning—United States.   I. Dick, Walter, 1937-   . II. Dick, Walter, 1937-   Planning effective instruction.   III. Title.
LB1028.38.R45   1996
375'.001—dc20   95-17021
                                                                          CIP

Printed in the United States of America

10 9 8 7 6 5   99

Contents

Preface

Our motivation for writing this book was to provide teachers with a set of instructional planning skills to develop more effective instructional practices with the eventual result of greater student achievement. These planning skills have been used with great success by people who systematically design instructional materials. However, our goal was not to teach teachers to become instructional designers but rather to have teachers use some of the procedures and techniques that designers use to create effective instruction. We have attempted to provide skills that can be applied realistically within elementary and secondary classrooms without any special equipment or aids.

This text can be used in any of several teacher preparation courses. It may be used in a generic introductory course, or it may be used in a content-specific teacher education course. In the latter case the instructor would supplement the examples provided in the text with those that are most appropriate to the content area in which the students will become teachers. Lastly, the text may be effectively used in courses for inservice teachers who are looking for a new perspective on their classroom teaching activities.

To make it easier to learn from our text, we have used a standard format for each chapter. This format is described in detail in Chapter 1.

Each chapter contains an Application section that describes activities for a cumulative project. We encourage consideration of these activities because the true strength of the ideas that are being presented is most apparent in their application. It is our belief that the best understanding of the concepts in this book will come about from their use.

We tried, in developing the first edition of this book, to be faithful to our own design model. Nowhere was this more important than in our use of tryout and revision procedures. After the initial draft of the book was completed, we used it in a variety of ways. First, we met each week with two undergraduate students who read and critiqued the text, chapter by chapter, with us. We acknowledge the insightful comments of Teresa Robson and Bill Perry, who certainly gave us a better look at the instructional design process from the point of view of preservice teachers.

In addition, Barbara Brinson and Catherine Price used a draft of the first edition with their students at Southern Methodist University and Valdosta State College, respectively. Their feedback, along with that of their students, was invaluable to us. We also want to thank the following reviewers who gave us detailed critiques of an early draft of the first edition: Joann Bush, Juanita Cox, Judith Duffield, Debby King, Jim Klein, Marty Tessmer, and Karyn Wellhousen-Pugh. We would also like to thank James Russell and William Coscarelli, both of whom provided us with useful suggestions for the second edition. These various reviews resulted in a text that was substantially changed in a number of ways—all of which we believe are for the better. We gratefully acknowledge the value of this feedback, while retaining responsibility for the errors of omission and commission that may remain.

Finally, we would like to thank Cindy Bigbee, Virginia Charles, Marcy Driscoll, Janette Hill, Elizabeth Kirby, Lane Lovell, Barbara Martin, Mary Ann Miller, Edna Mory, Jennifer Radford, Karen Rice, and Julie Woodworth, all of whom worked with us during the past five years as we conducted research examining the instructional planning practices of teachers. We hope that the insights we gained as a result of our research efforts have resulted in a book that will be of practical value to teachers.

Instructional Planning

Introduction

When you think about the duties teachers perform, what is the first thing that comes to your mind? When they attempt to answer this question, most people usually think about teachers in the classroom, either delivering instruction to students or guiding students as they engage in various activities. And, certainly, such activities are an important part of a teacher's job. However, another part of a teacher's job is equally important, and that involves the planning of instruction, that is, planning what the teacher and students will be doing in the classroom (and sometimes outside of the classroom). This book is designed to help you perform this important task.

What evidence do we have that planning is an important part of teaching? Many researchers have examined how teachers go about planning instruction, and a review of that research clearly shows that instructional planning plays a critical role in teaching and school learning (Clark & Dunn, 1991). Indeed, it has been stated that:

> Decisions made during planning have a profound influence on teachers' classroom behavior and on the nature and outcomes of education children receive. (Shavelson, 1983, p. 401)

When do teachers engage in planning? Contrary to the notion that teachers don't start planning their instruction until the night before they must present it, researchers have found that teachers are constantly engaged in planning. As one researcher put it, teachers plan their instruction "while driving home from school, while grocery shopping, [while] standing in the shower, [and while] sitting on the beach in July"

(McCutcheon, 1980). In other words, teachers are planning their instruction all the time!

Oftentimes, when we think about teachers planning their instruction, we think about them focusing on individual lessons and how they will teach those lessons. This type of planning, often referred to as *daily planning,* or *lesson planning,* certainly represents a large portion of teacher planning activities, However, teachers engage in many other "levels" of planning as well. These levels of planning include yearly planning, term planning, unit planning, and weekly planning.

In this book, we will focus most of our attention on planning the individual lesson or a series of related lessons. That is, when we discuss objectives, instructional activities, and assessment methods, we will be discussing how to plan them in relation to a single lesson or a group of related lessons. However, we will also touch upon unit, term, and yearly planning when we discuss such issues as identifying your instructional goals and implementing your instructional plan. More detailed discussions of long-range instructional planning may be found in other sources, such as texts on curriculum planning.

When teachers are engaged in instructional planning, what do you think they normally focus their attention upon? When they engage in long-range planning (yearly planning, term planning, and unit planning), they often focus on deciding the content (topics) that they will cover, the sequence in which those topics will be covered, and the amount of time they will spend on each topic. In many cases, the school district and/or state in which a teacher is working will already have made some of these decisions for the teacher, but even in these instances, the teacher is likely to focus much of his or her long-range planning on reviewing and fine-tuning such decisions.

After a teacher has decided upon such issues as the topics to be covered and the amount of time to be spent on each topic, the teacher will often turn his or her attention to the activities that will take place in the classroom. Indeed, researchers have found that the bulk of the short-term planning that most teachers engage in focuses on the identification of activities to use in the classroom.

A SYSTEMATIC APPROACH TO INSTRUCTIONAL PLANNING: AN INTRODUCTION

While we think that it is certainly necessary and appropriate for teachers to spend a good deal of planning time thinking about the instructional activities their students will engage in, we believe that before teachers do so, they should have a clear idea of what their goals are. Why is it important that teachers first be clear about their goals for students? Here's what one well-known educator, Robert Mager (1984), had to say about this matter: "If you're not sure where you're going, you're liable to end up someplace else."

We agree with the sentiment expressed by Mager; that is, we feel that *if you don't have a clear idea of what goals you have for your students, you will not be able to do a good job of planning instruction for them.* This notion, that instructional planning should usually begin with a clear picture of instructional goals, is one of the four key principles underlying the planning approach we will be describing in this book. Inasmuch as this approach starts with the identification of instructional goals and objectives, it has been referred to as an *objectives-first approach.* It has also been referred to as a *rational planning model* and as a *systematic approach* to instructional planning.

EFFECTIVE INSTRUCTION: THE END RESULT OF SYSTEMATIC PLANNING

The value of employing a systematic approach to instructional planning has been demonstrated in a wide variety of settings, ranging from school systems in developing countries (Morgan, 1989) to large corporations in the United States (Bowsher, 1989). In each case, it has been found that a systematic approach to instructional planning has resulted in effective instruction.

What do we mean by the term *effective instruction?* Effective instruction is instruction that enables students to acquire specified skills, knowledge, and attitudes. Effective instruction is also instruction that students enjoy.

How can we judge whether instruction is effective? If you reexamine our definition of effective instruction, you will see that we can't make a judgment based on what the teacher does. Rather, we must make a judgment based upon what students are able to do and how they feel as a result of the instruction they receive.

We can use a variety of ways to determine what students can do. For example, school districts often use standardized tests that have been developed by testing experts. At other times it is quite possible to use tests that have been developed by a local school district or by a classroom teacher. To determine how students feel about instruction, an important indicator is their reaction to questions we ask them about the instructional process.

Effective instruction is determined on the basis of data and information that are gathered and documented. It is not based upon casual observation of what might be going on in the classroom. Consider a type of elementary school teacher whom we have all known at some time during our years in school. This teacher often takes students on field trips to the mall and to other interesting local sites. The teacher provides lots of time at recess, often meets with parents and tells them how well their children are doing, and is generally acknowledged to be a very loving and supportive teacher. It is very difficult to be critical of a person like this, a teacher who seems to possess many of the qualities of a "good teacher."

However, it is also necessary to ask what students learn as a result of having spent a year with such a teacher. To what extent has their knowledge base increased? How many new skills have they acquired? Have they sharpened some of the skills they already possessed, and have their attitudes toward learning improved? If the answers to these questions can be documented in a positive fashion, we applaud such a teacher for having delivered effective instruction. If, however, there have been no changes in the level of student performance or attitudes, we have to wonder about the effectiveness of the instruction these students have received.

KEY PRINCIPLES UNDERLYING SYSTEMATIC INSTRUCTIONAL PLANNING

How does a teacher go about planning for effective instruction? One way of doing so is by employing the systematic approach to instructional planning that we referred to earlier.

What constitutes a systematic approach to instructional planning? What principles must be adhered to in order for us to agree that instruction was planned systematically? Different individuals will provide you with different answers to this question, but we believe that—at a minimum—in order to engage in systematic instructional planning, teachers (or anyone else involved in planning instruction) should adhere to four principles. Each of these principles is listed below:

1. Begin the planning process by clearly identifying the general goals and specific objectives students will be expected to attain;
2. Plan instructional activities that are intended to help students attain those objectives;
3. Develop assessment instruments that measure attainment of those objectives; and
4. Revise instruction in light of student performance on each objective and student attitudes towards your instructional activities.

A SYSTEMATIC PLANNING PROCESS

How does someone go about systematically planning instruction? There are many different methods for doing so, most of which incorporate the four principles described above. Some of these planning methods are quite complex, involving a great many steps. Others are much simpler. The

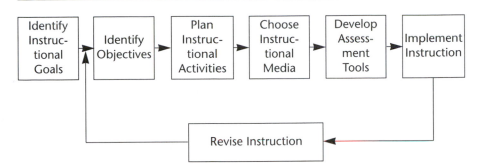

systematic planning process we recommend for teachers is a fairly simple one, comprised of seven steps. These steps are portrayed in Figure 1.1.

As indicated in Figure 1.1, the first step in our planning process involves identifying your instructional goals. An *instructional goal* is a general statement of what learners will be able to do as a result of instruction. Examples of instructional goals include:

- Students will be able to solve basic addition and subtraction problems.
- Students will demonstrate their knowledge of how the United States Congress operates.

After you identify your general goals, the next step involves your instructional objectives. These objectives will be specific statements of what students will be able to do at the end of your instruction. Typically, there are a number of objectives for each goal. If we were to develop some objectives based on the goals listed above, those objectives might include the following:

- Given two single-digit numbers, the student will add those two numbers correctly;
- Given a role as a legislator in a mock version of the United States Congress, the student will draft a piece of legislation and carry it through the processes necessary to turn it into a law.

Once you have identified where you want your students to go (as expressed via your goals and objectives), you can then start thinking about how to get them there. In other words, once you have identified what you would like your students to learn, you can start thinking about the instructional activities that will assist them in the learning process. Thus, the third step in our planning process requires you to identify the instructional activities you will employ with your students. These activities are the steps you will take when you present your students with instruction related to an objective or group of objectives.

In many cases, it is likely that your instructional activities will involve use of the "traditional" instructional media employed by teachers, namely the chalkboard, textbooks, workbooks, and other supplementary print materials. However, there are likely to be many other instances when you will want to use other instructional media. Thus, the fourth step in our model focuses on choosing instructional media.

When your students participate in the instructional activities, you will want to determine whether they learned what you expected them to learn. Therefore the fifth step in our planning process requires you to develop assessment tools designed to determine whether your students can demonstrate the skills, knowledge, and attitudes that you described in your objectives.

After your goals and objectives have been identified, and you have planned your instructional activities and your assessment techniques, you will be ready to try out, or implement, your instruction with your students. This is a very important step in the planning process because it provides you with information regarding the effectiveness of the instruction. That is, by trying out the materials with learners, you will get a picture of the extent to which students learn what you wanted them to learn. Indeed, it has been shown that without trying out instruction with students, educators often are unable to predict accurately the learning effectiveness of the instruction they plan.

The seventh and final step in our planning process involves revising instruction based upon the data you collect during the implementation phase. If, during that phase, you find that students are not learning what you wanted them to learn, and/or they are not enjoying the learning process, you will want to go back and try to revise some aspect of your instruction so as to better enable your students to accomplish their goals.

Does This Process Limit the Way You Go About Teaching?

The instructional planning process we will be describing does not presuppose any particular approach to teaching. It is based on one fundamental concept: that you are able to state your instructional goals in terms of what you expect your students to do after they have completed your instruction. If you are able to describe the learning outcomes you want your students to attain, then the rest of your plan will flow from those statements. And a great variety of instructional approaches can be employed in order to help your students attain these outcomes. It is important that we stress this flexibility in the planning process we are proposing. As you begin working through the process, please keep in mind that it is not a rigid plan, but rather one that allows for a variety of instructional approaches.

Are You Really Likely to Use This Planning Process?

If the process depicted in Figure 1.1 appears rather formidable, we would like to assure you that following such a process is not that difficult nor time-consuming after you have done it several times. Indeed, most teachers regularly make decisions about each of the steps in the process. Often, however, those decisions are not made in a systematic fashion. Our goal is to help you make those decisions systematically. Believe it or not, once you become accustomed to making instructional planning decisions systematically, you'll find that it won't take much time to do so!

Although in time you will find that our planning process is a simple one, we expect that when you first use it, it will be fairly time-consuming. Indeed, those individuals who have examined the planning practices of teachers have found that experienced teachers work from plans that are much sketchier than the detailed plans prepared by new teachers (Clark & Dunn, 1991). This is because experienced teachers have a much richer set of teaching experiences upon which they can draw as they go about planning their instruction. They often use these experiences to form mental images of what a lesson will be like. In contrast, the novice teacher lacks these experiences. By preparing detailed written plans, like those called for in this book, the novice teacher may begin to think about some of the instructional possibilities that are likely to come more readily to mind among experienced teachers.

As you become a more experienced teacher, it is quite likely that the written plans you develop will become much less detailed than the plans you prepared as a novice. However, we believe that by preparing detailed written plans at this point in your career, you will establish a firm planning base upon which you will be able to build less detailed plans in the future. A similar thought has been expressed by Clark and Peterson (1986), two researchers who conducted one of the most thorough reviews of how teachers go about planning their instruction. After completing their review, these researchers stated:

> It may be that training novice teachers in the use of a version of the rational planning model provides them with an appropriate foundation for developing a planning style compatible with their own personal characteristics and with the task environment in which they must teach. (p. 268)

We believe that the planning process described in this book will provide you with the firm foundation Clark and Peterson describe.

The Format of This Textbook

The chapters in this text all have a similar structure. Each chapter has seven major sections. Following a transition statement and a diagram of the planning process, the sections are

- Problem Scenario
- Chapter Objectives
- Background Information
- Major Concepts and Examples
- Practice and Feedback
- Application
- Summary

Problem Scenario

A description of a situation that is all too common in the teaching profession begins each chapter. Each teaching scenario can be addressed by applying the skills described in the chapter, and the situation in the scenario is discussed in later parts of the chapter.

Chapter Objectives

For each chapter there are several major objectives that are stated in terms of what you will be able to do as a result of having read and studied the chapter.

Background Information

This section includes information that helps to bridge the chapter with earlier chapters and describes related events in the field of education, which should help put the chapter into a larger framework. At times, a theoretical perspective is described.

Major Concepts and Examples

This is the most critical component of each chapter. Major ideas and concepts that apply to the objectives for the chapter are presented here along with examples. In some cases the examples involve descriptions of situations in which the concepts and ideas presented in the chapter are properly applied. In other cases, there are descriptions of improper applications. We point out the major differences between the two!

Practice and Feedback

In each chapter there are a variety of exercises directly related to the objectives of the chapter. After completing these exercises, you will be able to compare your responses with those provided in the feedback section.

Application

As you read this book, it will be most beneficial to develop an instructional plan of your own. The application section of each chapter guides you in developing a specific portion of your plan. By the time you finish this book, you will have developed and evaluated an entire instructional plan.

Summary

This section summarizes the major ideas that have been presented in the chapter.

At the back of this book there is a glossary that contains definitions of some of the key terms that we use. Many students have told us that they have found it to be a useful reference. Also at the back of the book are a bibliography and index that we hope you will find helpful.

SUMMARY

In this chapter we have indicated that instructional planning is a very important part of teaching; indeed, it is an activity that teachers engage in all the time! Teachers engage in a variety of types of instructional planning. During long-range planning (including yearly planning, term planning, and unit planning), they often focus on deciding the content (topics) that they will cover, the sequence in which those topics will be covered, and the amount of time they will spend on each topic. During short-range planning (weekly and daily planning), teachers often focus their attention on the identification of activities to use in the classroom.

We believe that before teachers begin thinking a lot about the instructional activities they would like to use, they should have a clear picture of the general goals and specific instructional objectives they would like their students to attain. This point of view is at the heart of the systematic planning process we will be describing in this book. The four key principles that underlie this process are:

1. Begin the planning process by clearly identifying the general goals and specific objectives students will be expected to attain;
2. Plan instructional activities that are intended to help students attain those objectives;
3. Develop assessment instruments that measure attainment of those objectives; and
4. Revise instruction in light of student performance on each objective and student attitudes towards your instructional activities.

We have described a seven-step systematic planning process. This process can be used to plan a variety of instructional approaches, ranging from teacher lectures to hands-on student-centered activities. Moreover, as a result of using this process, you should be able to develop effective instruction—instruction that enables students to learn and that students will enjoy.

If you are a novice teacher, it is likely that you will find that the planning process described in this book can be somewhat time-consuming and that it requires a good deal of written work. However, as you gain experience, you should find that this process becomes much simpler and that most of the planning can be done mentally rather than in writing. We believe that by preparing detailed written plans at this point in your career, you will establish a firm planning base upon which you will be able to build less detailed, but nonetheless effective, plans in the future.

C H A P T E R   2

Identifying Instructional Goals

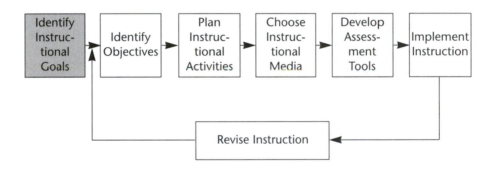

The systematic process for planning instruction always begins with the identification of instructional goals. What are instructional goals? How are they established and used? What sources can you turn to in order to help you identify instructional goals? This chapter examines these questions.

PROBLEM SCENARIO

Ms. Kittering has just been hired as a middle school language arts teacher. This is her first teaching position and she is just beginning to plan her instruction for the sixth-grade class she will be teaching. She would like to begin by identifying her instructional goals for this class. How might she go about doing so? What sources might she turn to, and what other information might be of use to her as she tries to identify these goals?

CHAPTER OBJECTIVES

The objectives for this chapter are that you will be able to:

1. describe the characteristics of instructional goal statements
2. describe how instructional goals are established
3. describe the uses of instructional goals
4. identify sources from which instructional goals may be derived
5. identify the student characteristics that you should consider as you go about planning your instruction, and describe how you can obtain information about those characteristics

BACKGROUND INFORMATION

We will use goal statements as the entry point for our planning process. Without instructional goals we are merely carrying out a random set of activities that may or may not be of benefit to learners. Because the goals we have for our educational programs are the starting points from which we derive all subsequent activities, they are crucial to the teaching/learning process.

Goals are derived from a number of sources and are expressed in a variety of ways. Consider, for example, the following situations that could occur in any school district. We might find administrators arguing the merits of academic skills versus vocational education for students. We might find a group of parents debating, in very loud terms, the pros and cons of introducing a new sex education program in the school district. We might find a group of teachers engaged in a discussion of the merits of a curriculum that stresses the growth and performance of the individual student as opposed to a curriculum that focuses upon the importance of cooperation in groups. And in a specific content area, such as elementary science, we might find the teachers debating the value of students doing experiments against the value of memorizing scientific facts.

Interest in establishing educational goals is not limited to parents, administrators, and teachers. As a result of their concerns for the educational process, state legislators often become involved in the process of goal setting. For example, you might find some legislators advocating that a certain number of hours be spent on writing essays in English classes or that the free enterprise system be stressed in social studies courses.

These situations are representative of the great variety of ways goals are established in the schools. Goal setting is critically important because goals determine, to a large part, what students experience in school and, to some extent, what teachers will actually teach. We will not be discussing a methodology for establishing educational goals. We simply recognize that goals *are* established in a variety of ways and by a variety of sources and that there is no single or correct set of educational goals. They are continually in transition.

MAJOR CONCEPTS AND EXAMPLES

Characteristics of Instructional Goal Statements

Instructional goal statements vary from one another in several different ways. They certainly differ in terms of specificity. For example, the statement "students will write effectively" is more general than the statement "students will write effective business letters," but both could be considered statements of an instructional goal. Goals may also differ in terms of their focus of action. For example, while some may describe what will be expected of students ("students will learn about our nation's past"), others focus on what teachers will do ("teach basic math skills") or what schools will try to accomplish ("all our students will be good citizens").

For our purposes, we will identify instructional goal statements as *general* statements of desired instructional outcomes that usually can be broken down into a variety of much more specific behaviors. Moreover, instructional goal statements should be expressed in terms of what is expected of the students (as opposed to what is expected of teachers).

While we won't use it as part of our definition, we would like to point out that instructional goal statements are less likely to be associated with short-term planning than they are with long-term planning. That is, instructional goals usually don't describe a specific behavior that a student will acquire in a relatively short period of time, such as during a single lesson or short unit of instruction; instead, they are more likely to describe a set of behaviors that students will acquire over a relatively longer period of time, perhaps over the course of a semester or one or more school years.

How Instructional Goals Are Established

The instructional goals for our schools are established in many different ways. Some are mandated through legislation. Others are established by accrediting agencies that insist students be able to perform a particular set of skills. Often, the local school board will affirm the goals established by the legislature and accrediting agencies and then place their own emphasis upon goals they feel are of greatest importance to the local school district.

In every school district there are special interest groups as well as parent/teacher organizations that attempt to influence the interpretation of educational goals and the instruction that is related to them. Similarly, teachers and curriculum supervisors and other administrators influence how the goals are implemented as they attempt to match goals to the curriculum.

Another major source of instructional goals is textbooks. Consider the role of a textbook in any curriculum. It can be argued that, in many teaching situations, the textbook serves as the curriculum. In this case, the goals of the curriculum and the goals expressed in the textbooks are one and the same. At the very least, we know that textbooks often play a major role in influencing what is taught in a course.

The ultimate consumer for any set of goals is the individual teacher. It is the teacher's responsibility to translate the goals into programs for learners and it is the interpretation of, and emphasis on, these goals that determines what is taught in the classroom. Teachers not only affect how goals are implemented; they can also help establish goals. That is, teachers may involve themselves at any of the levels described above to influence the groups that ultimately determine the goals for the curriculum. Therefore, it is important to be aware of both the origins of the goals and the potential range of views that will be held among the people who make up an educational community. Many of these views will ultimately be reflected in the goals of a school district and will eventually be translated into a curriculum and into instructional and testing processes in the classroom.

Uses of Instructional Goals

Goals are often used as the focus for developing a curriculum. For example, a state legislature has mandated that all students in the state must demonstrate mastery of basic skills in mathematics prior to graduating from the eighth grade. Around the state, this goal has not only influenced the content of mathematics programs, but science, home economics, and industrial arts programs as well.

In addition to serving as guides to curriculum development, goals serve a variety of other functions. For example, they can be used to inform the public of what a school or school district is trying to achieve. Goal statements such as "each student will have mastered basic mathematical skills prior to graduation from eighth grade" describe a school's priorities; such statements help the public determine the instructional emphasis in a school. A set of goal statements for a school district may also be used to determine the consistency of those goals with state mandates and guidelines set forth by accrediting agencies.

Goals also provide guidance for testing programs in schools. If schools are to be accountable for their goals, they must determine if their goals are being achieved. To do this, a testing program must be established that directly measures attainment of the established goals. In the example of a goal related to basic skills in mathematics, there must be a basic skills test in mathematics administered to all eighth grade students to determine if they have mastered these skills. In some states, both the goals and the corresponding tests are developed at the state level and provided to the districts for their use.

In the final analysis, the identification of goals provides direction for the instructional activities that take place in the classroom. That is why it is the first step in our systematic planning process.

Sources to Help You Identify Instructional Goals

How should you, as a teacher, go about identifying your instructional goals? Although you certainly can identify your own instructional goals and use them as the basis for your other planning decisions, it is important for you to realize that the local school, school district, and state in which you will work are likely to have identified a variety of instructional goals they will expect your students to accomplish. These instructional goals will appear in curriculum guides, teachers guides, and other planning materials prepared by local and state education agencies. It is likely that you will be given, or have access to, several of these documents when you become a teacher.

Textbooks are another printed source of educational goals. Oftentimes, the teacher's edition of a text will include a series of goals (and/or more specific objectives) the text is intended to help you accomplish. These goals may or may not be similar to the goals specified by your school, school district, or state.

In addition to these written sources of goals, your colleagues will be another source you may draw upon. The administrators, curriculum supervisors, and fellow teachers at your school and in your district certainly should be able to inform you of some instructional goals they think you should be working toward. Your former professors may help as well. In each of these cases, however, the goals expressed by these individuals may or may not match the goals listed in the other sources we have talked about.

Given that the instructional goals you identify may differ depending upon the source(s) from which you derive them, a large part of the decision as to which goals to focus upon will be up to you. However, you should be careful not to ignore any state or local mandates concerning instructional goals.

Student Characteristics and Instructional Goals

As you go about identifying your instructional goals and the other portions of your instructional plans, it is very important that you consider the characteristics of your students. Why? Because it is clear that in any school there is a wide range of differences among students in the various classes; and even within classes, large individual differences among the students are likely to exist. Recognition of these differences will be important in determining whether or not your instruction will be effective.

There are a variety of a questions you can ask about your students that will help you to plan more effective instruction. These questions include the following:

- What is the general ability level of your students?
- What skills and knowledge are they bringing to the instructional situation?
- What attitudes do they have, not only toward what you are teaching but also toward learning in general?

Information of this sort is of great importance in developing your instruction plans.

As you go about setting your instructional goals, information about the general ability level of your students is particularly important. In this text, we will be considering students who are grouped into three categories of ability levels. Those categories are often labeled *above average, average,* and *below average,* or *learning disabled.* Like any labels, these categories mask many differences within the groups, and often children placed in one group might be better served by being in another group. However, schools frequently place students within these categories on the basis of IQ tests. For example, students with IQs of 130 or above are often considered above average, if not gifted, and those with IQs below 90 are often considered below average. We do not consider these labels to be very important, but we do think it is important that you think about the actual differences in general ability levels among students as you develop your instructional goals and subsequent plans.

How do you go about getting information about the ability level of your students? School records often contain information about students' IQ scores and student performance on other measures of general ability. Previous teachers can also provide you with test scores and personal observations about your students, both of which can help give you a clearer picture of the students' general abilities. These teachers may also be able to provide you with information about your students' attention spans, areas of interest, and cooperative and disruptive behavior patterns, all of which can help you plan your instructional activities. We will review this point in greater detail when we discuss instructional activities in Chapter 4.

Although it certainly is important to be aware of the general abilities and attitudes of your students, perhaps the most important data you can gather about your students is information about the specific skills and knowledge they possess in a particular content area. Oftentimes, you can gather such information through the use of pretests and other less formal techniques of assessing your students. Information gathered through such means will be particularly helpful as you go about identifying the specific objectives you would like your students to attain. This matter will be discussed in detail in the next chapter of this book.

Ms. Kittering's Dilemma

At the beginning of this chapter, we indicated that Ms. Kittering was trying to identify instructional goals for her sixth-grade language arts class. How should she go about doing so? She might begin by reviewing whatever instructional planning materials (curriculum guides, teacher's guides, etc.) she has at her disposal, as well as by examining the goals stated or implied in the textbook she will be using. Discussions with the other sixth-grade language arts teachers at her middle school might also be helpful. In addition, if the school or district has a middle school language arts curriculum supervisor, it might be worthwhile for Ms. Kittering to have a discussion with that person.

As she goes about identifying her instructional goals, Ms. Kittering should also be thinking about the characteristics of the students who will be in her class. She may want to ask previous teachers about the general abilities, skills, attitudes, and interests of these students. School records may also provide her with some information. In addition, she may get a general sense of her students' characteristics by asking her fellow teachers about the characteristics of previous sixth-grade classes that may be similar to the class she will be teaching. Finally, at the beginning of the new semester, Ms. Kittering should spend some time "getting to know" her students, both through formal (e.g., pretesting) and informal means. The information she gathers via these techniques is likely to be useful as she goes about making a variety of instructional planning decisions.

PRACTICE

Listed below are three sets of questions. After you have answered the questions, compare your answers with the suggested answers in the feedback section that follows.

1. Describe four important sources of instructional goals. Indicate which source you believe is most important.
2. From the standpoint of instructional planning, what is the most important use of instructional goals?

3. Listed below are a number of possible instructional goals. Indicate which ones are described in terms of student behaviors.

   A. All students will be treated alike.
   B. Students will be able to write effectively.
   C. Students will have an outstanding school.
   D. Students will be able to engage in good health habits.
   E. Promote student loyalty to the community.

FEEDBACK

1. There are many sources of instructional goals, and it is very difficult to single out one as being the most important. Perhaps you mentioned *parents*. Parents certainly are an important source of goals, but the way they influence goals is often through their *school boards, school administrators,* and *state legislatures.* State legislatures establish the mandatory goals for schools, while local school boards provide their own interpretation and add a local dimension to those goals. And, of course, *teachers* play an important role in the goal-setting process, primarily in terms of determining which goals will be emphasized in the classroom. You may have also noted that the *textbook* chosen for a course may become a source for goal statements. In addition to these sources, *accrediting agencies* and *special interest groups* also have an important influence on the setting of instructional goals.

2. Although statements of goals serve many purposes in communicating to the community what it is schools are attempting to accomplish, for our purposes the most important function goals serve is that they are the starting point for determining what and, to a certain extent, how content will be taught in the classroom.

3. The goals stated in terms of student behaviors are (b), "all students will be able to write effectively" and (d), "students will be able to engage in good health habits." The other three alternatives do not directly involve student behavior. Choice (a), "all students will be treated alike," is not a student learning outcome. It appears to be a description of how teachers are to treat students. Choice (c), "students will have an outstanding school," is certainly important, but it's too vague a statement to serve as a goal from which instructional practices could be derived. Alternative (e), "promote student loyalty to the community," describes a goal for the school, but doesn't really indicate how the students would display that loyalty to the community.

APPLICATION

The application section of each chapter includes suggestions for a project that you might undertake. The project is one that you will work on as you proceed through this book. It will begin with the identification of a set of goals and proceed through the planning of an actual lesson which will be implemented in a classroom and revised. In each subsequent chapter you will learn how to do a part of the instructional planning process.

To begin the project, write several goals related to your own area of interest and expertise. If you do not feel confident about using a particular academic content area, consider a special hobby or interest that you have that others might want to learn about. The goals should focus on what students will be able to do and not on what a teacher or school will be attempting to accomplish.

The goals you prepare for this assignment will serve as the basis for additional activities you will conduct in subsequent chapters. Choose your goals carefully and make sure that they are in areas in which you have sufficient knowledge to develop instruction.

SUMMARY

In this chapter we have defined instructional goals as general statements of desired instructional outcomes that usually can be broken down into a variety of much more specific behaviors. We have also indicated that instructional goals may be expressed in terms of what is expected of the school, teacher, or student and that instructional goals are often associated with long-term instructional planning.

Instructional goals are established in a variety of ways. State legislatures, accrediting agencies, and local school boards often mandate that schools focus on particular goals. Special interest groups, parents, school administrators, and teachers also influence the establishment and implementation of school goals. Furthermore, to the extent that they affect what is taught in a class, textbooks also influence school goals.

Instructional goals are used for several purposes. They serve as a means of informing the general public, as well as various governmental and private agencies, of the areas of instructional emphasis within a school or district. These goals also serve as a focus for curriculum and test development. As such, they are a logical starting point for most instructional planning efforts.

There are a variety of sources from which teachers can derive their instructional goals. These sources include curriculum guides, teachers guides, and other planning materials prepared by local and state education agencies. In addition, textbooks, school administrators, curriculum supervisors, and fellow teachers can help teacher identify their instructional goals.

Teachers should identify their instructional goals in light of the characteristics of their students. The general ability level of students, as well as their skills, knowledge, interests, and attitudes, should be taken into consideration as a teacher decides upon instructional goals and makes other instructional planning decisions. Information about these characteristics may be obtained from school records and previous teachers, as well as from assessing students through the use of pretests and other less formal means.

Identifying Objectives

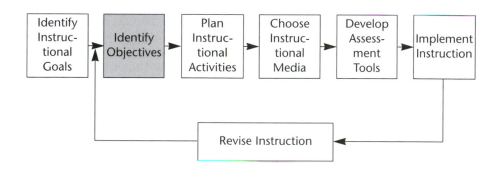

As we discussed in the previous chapter, *instructional goals* are general statements of desired instructional outcomes that can usually be broken down into much more specific behaviors. *Objectives* describe those specific behaviors. They are explicit descriptions of what students will be able to do as a result of the instruction they receive. In this chapter, we will discuss why specifying objectives is an important part of the planning process. We will then describe a system for classifying different types of objectives. After we have presented you with a picture of what objectives are, we will discuss how you may derive objectives from instructional goals, and we will also discuss other considerations (such as the characteristics of your students) in choosing and describing your objectives.

PROBLEM SCENARIO #1

The teachers in the English department in a local high school are examining the school district's goals in their area with the intent of translating those goals into specific instructional objectives for learners. They have just encountered the following goal: Students will be able to write effectively.

A lively discussion has taken place. What does it mean to write effectively? Does it mean that all of the students can write an essay? If so, how good must that essay be? Would being able to write a simple note that conveys information accurately be sufficient? How will students demonstrate that they have effectively achieved this goal? How do we get from very general goals to statements of specific skills that students should achieve?

PROBLEM SCENARIO #2

One of the objectives Ms. Helmer has for her low-ability eighth grade class is that they will be able to compute percentages. The state has mandated this as a skill for all the students at the eighth grade level. In her introductory lesson, Ms. Helmer defined what a percentage is and then used the blackboard to show the students how to solve a number of percentage problems. However, she found that the students were puzzled and unable to answer her questions about the procedures for computing percentages. When she passed out a worksheet, almost none of the students were able to begin solving the problems. Clearly, Ms. Helmer and the students have a problem. What would you suggest with regard to the objective the students are trying to achieve?

CHAPTER OBJECTIVES

The objectives for this chapter are that you will be able to:

1. identify objectives that are written in correct three-component form
2. classify various objectives according to the domain of learning they represent
3. write objectives for various instructional goals
4. write shortened objectives for objectives written in correct three-component form
5. identify appropriate prerequisites for given objectives
6. describe how objectives may be modified on the basis of students' knowledge, skills, and attitudes

BACKGROUND INFORMATION

The use of objectives in education has been advocated for many years. Perhaps the person who is best known in this regard is Robert Mager, who popularized the notion of behavioral objectives. Mager's point of view was that to develop a teaching plan, we had to know exactly what the students would be able to do when they completed our instruction. He argued that before we ever begin to develop instruction, we must state our objectives in terms of student outcomes. These objectives then guide the rest of the instructional process.

This emphasis on the development of objectives became very controversial. There were those who strongly endorsed Mager's efforts to specify clearly those things that were to be learned by students. However, there were others who said that the use of behavioral objectives was very detrimental. They argued that because we only stated very specific observable behaviors in objectives, we often ended up only writing objectives about the most trivial outcomes of education. Furthermore, critics felt that things inside the learner which we couldn't see were the important changes that were taking place. In addition, they argued that the behavioral objectives essentially dictated the curriculum and the things teachers could do at any given time. Objectives, they said, removed the possibility of taking advantage of "teachable moments" in the classroom, those moments that would spontaneously arise and provide teachers with an opportunity to teach students something that was possibly outside the range of the normal curriculum. Critics of objectives argued that if teachers strictly adhered to teaching by objectives, they would ignore those "teachable moments."

Although many of these types of arguments and beliefs concerning behavioral objectives exist to this day, an increasing number of teachers are finding objectives to be useful. Teachers realize that objectives can guide and increase the effectiveness of the instructional process and serve as a means of communicating to students, parents, administrators, and other educators what it is that they are trying to achieve in the classroom. Many teachers now realize that objectives do not necessarily limit the instructional methods they use or prevent them from capitalizing upon "teachable moments." Instead, objectives help teachers to focus upon the outcomes of instruction and enable them to recognize whether their students have attained those outcomes.

MAJOR CONCEPTS AND EXAMPLES

Objectives are explicit descriptions of what *students* will be able to do as a result of the instruction they receive (we have emphasized the word *student* so that you won't make the common mistake of writing an objective in terms of what a teacher will do). Each objective describes a specific *observable* behavior a student should be able to perform. An observable behavior is an action that we can actually see the learner perform and oftentimes results in an observable product, such as an essay or a list of names.

In order for an objective to describe an observable behavior, it must include an action verb, a verb that describes an observable action in which a learner will engage. Examples of such verbs include *explain, list, climb, spell, describe, identify, rotate,* and so on.

Conversely, objectives should not include verbs that describe internal mental states that are not directly observable. Examples of such verbs include *know, understand,* and *appreciate.* These verbs, and others like them, do not describe observable behaviors. Instead they describe internal mental states that mean different things to different people. For example, how can you tell whether a student "knows" the concept *democracy?* Does the student know the concept if the student can define what the term *democracy* means? How about if the student can name several countries that have democratic forms of government? Or perhaps the student should be able to tell us whether a particular form of government we describe is a democracy. If our objective is that a student "knows" the concept of democracy, it is important that we are clear about which behavior we want the student to exhibit.

We do not want you to get the impression that we think that such mental processes as thinking and appreciating are unimportant. Quite the contrary! These are the essence of education. We, as teachers, must help students process information effectively and become effective problem solvers. However, the only way we can observe how effective we have been is by observing and assessing the results of the use of these processes. The only way we can tell whether a student knows, understands, or appreciates something is to have the student *do something* to demonstrate that knowledge, understanding, or appreciation. It is that "something" (be it defining a term, identifying examples of a term, or something else), which we need to specify in an objective.

Components of an Objective

An objective typically consists of three basic components. The first describes the actual *behavior* we expect our students to exhibit as a result of instruction. Examples of such behaviors would include writing the names of the capitals of various states, determining the answers to various multiplication problems, identifying examples of reptiles, setting up a television camera, and choosing to throw trash in a litter basket rather than on the ground. As you can see, this is the portion of the objective in which the action verb appears.

The second component of an objective is a description of the *conditions* under which the student will be required to exhibit the desired behavior. For example, if students are expected to describe the strengths and weaknesses of Article I of the Constitution, will they be required to recall, from memory, the provisions of that Article, or will they be allowed to refer to a copy of Article I as they attempt to describe its strengths and weaknesses? In the first case, the conditions would be stated: "Without any reference materials, the student will . . ." In the latter case, the conditions would be: "Given a copy of Article I of the Constitution, the student will . . ."

If students must draw a circle, will they be able to use a compass or must they draw it freehand? In solving a number of numerical problems, will students be able to use their calculators or will they be required to do their own computations? Each of these questions focuses upon what will be available to students when they are performing the behavior described in an objective. In other words, the questions focus upon the conditions under which a behavior will be performed. By asking yourself, "what will be available to students at the time I assess their performance?" you will be able to identify the conditions portion of your objectives.

It is important to note that the conditions portion of an objective does not include such statements as "after listening to my instructions" or "after going through the workbook" or "after studying the reading package." An objective does not state how the learner will acquire a new skill or knowledge, it simply indicates the conditions under which it will be performed after it has been taught.

The third and final component of an objective is referred to as the *criterion* or *standard* that must be met in order for the performance to be judged acceptable. Perhaps the standard you are most familiar with is that a test score of 90 percent and above is an A, 80 through 89 percent is a B, and so on. This standard indicates, in a very general way, the level of performance a student must attain in order to receive a particular grade.

The standards described in an objective are specific to the behavior described in that objective. For example, an objective might indicate that the student must correctly solve three out of four problems or must correctly list four out of five titles. Other examples of standards would be that a student would make no more than three errors while performing a procedure or that a student would choose a particular course of action in at least two out of three opportunities.

In addition to describing how well a student will be expected to perform a behavior, a standard may describe how quickly the student will be expected to perform it. For example, a standard may indicate that a student must be able to perform a certain skill, such as solving a physics problem, within a period of ten minutes.

Table 3.1 summarizes our discussion of the function of each component of an objective.

TABLE 3.1:   The Function of the Components of an Objective

Component	Function
Behavior	describes what the student will be expected to do (i.e., the observable action the student will be expected to take) as a result of instruction
Conditions	describes the circumstances (conditions) under which the student will be expected to perform the behavior; describes what the student will use when demonstrating the ability to perform the objective
Standards	describes how well (and perhaps how quickly) the student will be expected to perform the behavior

Sample Objectives

Now let's examine some objectives to determine their strengths and weaknesses. For example, consider this objective: "Without the use of any materials, the student will be able to list the titles of five Shakespearean plays. All five titles must be exactly correct." You should note several things about this objective. The first is that students are to perform this objective "without the use of any materials." Second, note that the objective actually contains two sentences. The standard, that all the titles must be exactly correct, is stated in a separate sentence. This is perfectly appropriate. Sometimes an objective can be communicated more clearly by breaking it into two or three sentences.

Here is another objective: "With a partner in a kneeling position, the student will execute the takedown hold according to the procedure described in the wrestling textbook." This is an objective in which the criterion for performance depends, in part, upon the instructor's judgment. It is clear that the student is to execute a particular wrestling hold from a starting position as described in the text, but how will the instructor judge whether the hold has been properly executed? At the very least, the instructor should have a checklist of the steps that should be performed when executing a takedown hold. The checklist could be in his or her head or, better yet, the instructor could prepare a brief written checklist to judge whether each student executed the takedown hold properly. It is usually wise to develop a brief checklist of the sequence of steps to properly execute any motor skill. By using such a checklist, an instructor may be better able to judge objectively whether a particular motor skill has been performed properly.

Let's look at another type of objective: "Given the opportunity to cheat by copying from another student, the student will choose not to cheat 100 percent of the time." We can see the three components of the objective here: "given the opportunity to cheat by copying from another student" would be the conditions; "choose not to cheat" would be the behavior; and the standard is "100 percent of the time." Although this objective includes the three major components, we would have difficulty in determining whether our students consistently behave in this fashion outside the classroom. At best, perhaps we can judge whether a student fails to achieve the objective by observing the cheating that takes place in the classroom. The general point to be made here is that while your goals can focus on behaviors that take place outside the classroom, most of your objectives should focus on behaviors you can observe while your students are in school.

Now let's turn to what we consider to be the "universal objective." It's universal because it covers almost all behaviors at all times, but says absolutely nothing. Consider this objective: "Given a multiple choice test, the student will circle the correct answer to nine of ten questions." This objective certainly contains a set of conditions, namely, "given a multiple choice test." The behavior is to circle the answers, and the standard is to answer nine of ten questions correctly. We have an objective that meets all of the criteria for an objective, but the objective describes absolutely nothing about the content or substance of the real behavior we are interested in. When you write your objectives, be careful that you describe the content of the behavior you want to see and don't fall into the trap of writing a "universal objective."

Domains of Learning

If you reexamine the first two sample objectives just described, you will note that they represent two very different types of learning outcomes. The first objective ("list the titles of five Shakespearean plays") requires the student to recall some information. In contrast, the second objective ("execute the takedown hold") requires the student to perform a physical activity.

The fact that these two objectives require two very different types of behavior is not at all unusual. Objectives can describe a variety of types of behaviors. A famous learning theorist, Robert Gagne, has developed a scheme, or *taxonomy,* that can be used to classify most objectives into one of four types, or *domains,* of learning outcomes. These domains of learning include *knowledge, intellectual skills, motor skills,* and *attitudes.* The strategies you use to help your students attain a particular objective usually vary depending upon the domain of learning the objective represents. Therefore, being able to distinguish among the various domains will be important when you plan instructional activities to help your students achieve your objectives. The following analysis should provide you with the information you need in order to distinguish among the four domains of learning outcomes.

Knowledge

Learning outcomes in the domain we call *knowledge* deal directly with the ability to recall and remember specific information. It's the kind of learning required of students when we ask them to learn the capitals of the states, the names of the presidents, or the symbols for the chemical elements. We usually refer to these sorts of tasks as memorization and, in some settings, a great deal of instruction is directed toward facilitating memorization of specific information.

Intellectual Skills

Intellectual skills are those processes used by students that go above and beyond the pure memorization of information to the actual use of the information. Almost every course in the public school curriculum emphasizes, to a greater or lesser extent, a variety of intellectual skills that students must learn. Just as intellectual skills are different from motor skills or knowledge, there are also different levels of these intellectual skills. It is important to be aware of these levels.

The lowest level of intellectual skill is that of *concept learning.* In simple terms, a *concept* is a label used to describe a group of related things or ideas. When we say that a student "understands" or has learned a concept, we mean that he or she is able to identify correctly whether a particular thing or idea can be classified as an example of that concept. For example, if a student "understands" the concept of a chair, he or she should be able to indicate whether or not a particular item is a chair.

The ability to understand various concepts is an important intellectual skill. Teachers spend a great deal of time teaching young children about concepts such as color, democracy, space, and so on. The importance of learning about concepts is not limited, however, to elementary school children. At the high school level, we get involved in teaching students about more complex concepts, such as electrons and ions. The task for the student is to use the parameters of what constitutes an electron to determine if particular examples are, in fact, electrons.

A second, and higher, level of intellectual skills is *rule using. Rules* are combinations of concepts. For example, the Pythagorean theorem states that "the length of the hypotenuse of a right triangle equals the square root of the sum of the squares of the length of the other two sides." In order to use this rule, learners must understand each of the concepts that are part of it, such as what is meant by square root, hypotenuse, and right triangle. Simply stating or writing the theorem is not an example of rule using. That is knowledge. The rule must actually be applied and the result determined in order to say that a student is using a rule.

The third and highest level of intellectual skills is *problem solving.* As in the case of rule using, when students engage in problem solving, they apply rules to help them solve problems. The distinction between problem solving and rule using is that in rule using, the student is asked to correctly use a given rule, whereas in *problem solving,* the student is given a problem to solve and must choose and correctly use the appropriate rules to solve the problem. In the former case, the student may be asked to use the Pythagorean theorem to determine the length of the side of a triangle, while in the latter the student may be asked to generate a solution to the problem of what to do with our garbage.

Motor Skills

Any physical activity that requires movement of all or part of the body is referred to as a *motor skill.* We are not referring to acts such as pushing a button, but rather more complex physical activities such as those involved in dancing, creating crafts, playing the piano, or throwing a football. Motor skills can be learned in the context of individual activities or team activities and are an important part of the public school curriculum.

Attitudes

The personal feelings and beliefs that result in a person's tendency to act in a particular way are referred to as *attitudes.* We often refer to someone's attitude about some topic or activity such as the environment; when we do so, we are usually referring to their general tendency to respond in a particular way with regard to the environment. One of the major goals of education is to shape the attitudes of the learners so that they will make responsible choices throughout their lives.

Table 3.2 provides a brief summary of information about each of the four domains of learning.

TABLE 3.2: Types (Domains) of Learning

Type (Domain) of Learning	Type of Behavior Learner is Expected to Perform	Sample Objective (Abbreviated)
Knowledge	recall information (facts)	recite the Gettysburg Address
Intellectual Skills		
Concept learning	identify examples of a concept	classify various types of chemical reactions
Rule Using	use a given rule to solve a particular type of problem	solve two-digit addition problems
Problem Solving	select and use the correct rules to solve a given problem	create a persuasive essay on the topic of gun control
Motor Skill	perform a physical activity	drill holes in wood with an electric drill
Attitude	exhibit behavior consistent with a given attitude	choose to recycle trash

It may be helpful to review some verbs that can be used to describe student behavior in the various domains of learning outcomes we have discussed. If you have an objective in the knowledge domain, then the behavior you are asking a student to perform basically is to list or state or to describe something from memory, or, perhaps, to recognize items from a list of things that the student has learned before.

If your objective is in the intellectual skills domain, then in all likelihood you are asking students to demonstrate their knowledge of concepts, rules, or problem-solving strategies. The corresponding verbs for these types of behaviors are to *classify* (concepts), to *apply* (rules), and to *solve* (problems).

In the motor skill domain you are nearly always asking students to either *perform* or *execute* some routine that they have already learned.

In the attitude domain we always use the word *choose* because we are asking students to reflect their feelings and beliefs by choosing a particular behavior to be exhibited. Here we are using the word *choose* not in the multiple-choice sense of that word, as when a student must choose the correct answer, but rather in terms of choosing some behavior from an array of possible behaviors. It is assumed that choosing a behavior that is appropriate for a particular setting reflects the student's real feelings and beliefs about that setting.

Suggested Verbs for Instructional Objectives

Domain of Learning Outcome	*Suggested Verbs*
Knowledge	List, state, describe, recognize
Intellectual Skills	Classify, apply, solve
Motor Skills	Perform, execute
Attitudes	Choose

Listed above are the verbs we suggest you use. You may find these verbs helpful as you write objectives for goals that you have identified. However, do not feel that only these verbs can be used to develop an acceptable objective. These are only suggestions. It is more important to state objectives in a way that is meaningful to you, and subsequently meaningful to learners, than it is to state objectives in a more stylized fashion that does not, in fact, represent what you mean.

Deriving Objectives from Goals

Now that you have an understanding of what objectives are and how they may be classified, we need to examine their role in the systematic planning process. In the previous chapter, we stated that a teacher should begin this process by identifying his or her instructional goals. The second step in this process involves identifying the specific objectives related to those goals.

How do we get from goal statements to specific objectives? Oftentimes, those objectives are provided for teachers. The same curriculum guides, teachers guides, textbooks, and other planning documents that we listed as sources of goals often list specific objectives as well. In such cases, you should check to see if those objectives are representative of the goals your students are expected to attain. In other instances, however, you will not be provided with objectives, in which case you will have to derive them from the goals you have identified. Let's look at an example of how you might go about this process.

Assume that we have the goal: "The students will develop appropriate life-long health habits." We could convert that into many specific objectives. Some of those objectives might be "list the major bones in the leg," "demonstrate appropriate techniques for brushing teeth," "diagnose appropriately when to go to a doctor," and "choose to use drugs appropriately." Are the behaviors described in these objectives representative of our goal?

Before we answer the question we have raised, note two things about the objectives that have been described here. First of all, they are written in brief form and are not complete objectives. Second, note that each of the four objectives represents a different domain of learning outcome. Thus we have an example of a goal that has resulted in objectives in the four different domains. As noted earlier, this is not unusual. A good way to derive objectives from a goal would be to think of appropriate objectives in each domain.

Now let's examine whether the objectives we identified are appropriate in light of our goal. In order to develop appropriate life-long health habits, is it really important for our students to be able to "list the major bones in the leg"? Probably not, and therefore we probably should delete this objective because it is unrelated to our goal of developing appropriate life-long health habits.

The other three objectives we identified in relation to our goal seem to be more appropriate. Choosing a drug-free lifestyle and being able to determine correctly when to go to the doctor certainly seem to be behaviors related to developing good life-long health habits. Being able to brush one's own teeth properly also is important, but you might question whether that is a behavior that should be assessed in school. That point is certainly debatable, and the answer depends, in part, on the age and mental capabilities of the learners.

The teachers in the English department who were described in the first problem scenario at the beginning of this chapter would have to go through a similar process to identify specific objectives for the goal of writing effectively. In this particular example, it is possible to generate a wide range of intellectual skills objectives. It would also be important to consider any attitudes that should be developed with regard to writing. After the objectives have been generated it would be important to compare them with lists of state and district competencies and with objectives in popular texts. With this information, plus information about the skills and attitudes of the students, it would be necessary to reduce the list to those that are of greatest importance and relevance to the students. This may require a long, but important, dialogue among teachers.

Limiting the Number of Objectives

As indicated in the examples described above, it is sometimes possible to derive many objectives from a single goal. What problems may arise if you do so? First, you may identify many more objectives than you could possibly cover. Second, by continuing to break goals and objectives down into their component skills, you may end up with a set of objectives that describe very minute (and often trivial) learning outcomes. How can you avoid such problems? The most obvious (and logical!) solution is to limit the number of objectives you identify.

Earlier, we indicated that instructional goals are often expected to be accomplished over a fairly long period of time, such as a semester or one or more school years. In contrast, it is may be useful to think of objectives as outcomes that students can attain in a relatively short period of time, such as by the end of a lesson or a series of related lessons. If you limit yourself to identifying one or two meaningful (as opposed to trivial) objectives that you would like your students to attain by the end of a lesson or lesson series, you are likely to avoid the pitfalls described in the previous paragraph.

Uses of Objectives

The instructional goal we referred to earlier was that students would develop appropriate life-long health habits. Developing instructional activities for a goal such as this, or nearly any goal, is difficult. Goals, by their very nature, are usually broad and general and sometimes rather vague. Objectives, however, are more specific and therefore serve as a better basis for planning instructional activities. In later chapters we will show you how to use your objectives as the basis for planning the instruction you will present to your students.

While objectives serve to describe what students will be able to do when they finish some instruction and to guide the planning of instruction, they also serve a number of other useful purposes. Teachers can, and should, use objectives to help them design tests. We will talk about using objectives for this purpose in Chapter 5. Teachers can share their objectives with their students to let them know what they will be expected to learn. In addition, objectives are very valuable for administrators as a way to relate the school curriculum to state and district standards and to communicate with others about their curriculum. Finally, objectives are very useful when talking with parents about what students are learning.

Short Forms of Objectives

Have you noticed that the stated objectives for our chapters are not complete, three-component objectives? We often omit the conditions and the criteria from our objectives and simply state the behaviors that we expect you to learn.

This manner of describing the objectives was a deliberate decision on our part and was done to communicate to you, the learner, the importance of the behaviors we hope to teach. It is a good idea to write all three components of an objective when you are planning your instructional activities and designing your tests. However, it is often easier to communicate your objectives to others (particularly your students) by dropping either the conditions or the standards from your objectives and simply describing the behaviors you would like to see attained.

Let's look at objectives in the four domains and see to what extent they might be shortened in order to simplify the communication of the behaviors in the objectives. In the knowledge domain, it is usually important to state the conditions under which the behavior will be demonstrated. We need to know whether students will be able to use aids to help them recall information (e.g., "Given the names of the Presidents of the United States, the student will list them in the order in which they served"), or whether the information must be memorized (e.g., "Without any aids, the student will name the Presidents of the United States in the order in which they served"). The exact standard that students must meet when they are recalling information is often not necessary. Therefore, when you are communicating knowledge objectives to your students, a statement of the behavior and conditions will often suffice.

For intellectual skills, the conditions under which the skill will be demonstrated often are implied. For example, being able to multiply whole numbers implies that the student will be given a set of whole-number multiplication problems. Thus, stating that the students will be given these problems is unnecessary. If, however, students will be allowed to use a calculator to solve the problems, this fact should be indicated. As was the case with knowledge objectives, it often seems unnecessary to include your standards. For intellectual skills objectives, you may choose to provide only a statement of the behavior in which you are interested.

For motor skills, the conditions are often implied, but it is usually important to describe the standard against which a skill will be judged.

By providing your students with standards, you will give them an indication of the precision and speed with which you expect them to perform a motor skill.

In the attitude domain, you will usually be asking your students to choose to act in a particular manner under a given set of circumstances. Thus, it often is necessary to indicate the conditions under which that choice will have to be made. It seems less important, however, to describe the standard you will use to judge your students' attainment of objectives in this domain.

Short Forms of Objectives

Domain of Learning Outcome	Components Usually Included
Knowledge	Conditions, Behavior
Intellectual Skills	Behavior
Motor Skills	Behavior, Standard
Attitudes	Conditions, Behavior

Discussing the short form of objectives is not common. Most references stick very closely to the concept of a three-component objective: conditions, behavior, and standard. However, we believe you must be flexible when you use objectives. If communication can be improved by making an objective less cumbersome, we think you should do so. This is no substitute, however, for knowing what you want students to be able to do. For the purposes of planning instruction and designing tests, all three components of an objective should be explicit and well understood. However, when that same objective is being described to others, the various short forms indicated above may be used to facilitate communication.

Learner Characteristics and Objectives: A Dilemma

In the previous chapter, we indicated that as you go about developing your instructional plans, it is very important that you consider the characteristics of your students. This is certainly true as you identify your objectives. Indeed, by thinking about your objectives in light of your students' characteristics, you will confront a problem that we believe teachers should not ignore.

The dilemma we are referring to involves the following question: Will you be teaching students or will you be teaching content? This question often perplexes teachers. On the one hand, teachers are confronted with a set of state or local objectives that are to be achieved by *all* their students; on the other hand, not all the students in a teacher's class are alike; the students in a particular class may vary greatly in terms of their learning abilities.

It is apparent that at times a teacher will be forced to take the attitude that he or she will teach content and those students who are capable of learning the content will do so and others will simply not be able to. Nonetheless, the teacher will have covered the content as outlined in the text or stated in the district objectives.

There will be other times, however, when a teacher may simply decide that it is not possible for the students who are in the class to master all the content that is supposed to be covered. Therefore, the teacher may proceed to make adjustments to the objectives for the class in order to bring the objectives into alignment with the capabilities of the students.

There is no one best answer to this dilemma. We would all like to find ourselves in a situation in which we are able to teach successfully all the content—the skills, knowledge, and attitudes—that students will need. Although this goal may not be totally attainable, in a subsequent chapter we will present an approach to teaching—the mastery approach—that attempts to adjust the instructional procedures used with students so that each student can attain the skills, knowledge, and attitudes we want them to achieve. In this chapter, we will describe ways of analyzing the abilities of our students and indicating how objectives might be modified in order to be more consistent with their abilities.

Prerequisite Skills: An Important Type of Learner Characteristic

Just as it is important to specify your objectives because they are statements that tell you where your students are going, it is equally important for you to know where your students are starting. Usually this starting point is referred to as their *prerequisite skills,* that is, the skills, knowledge, and attitudes that students must have in order to comprehend your instruction.

You are probably most familiar with the term *prerequisite* in connection with college courses that have prerequisites. Often the prerequisites are listed as other courses, but seldom are they listed in terms of specific knowledge or experience you must have before beginning a course. Nearly all of us have had the experience of taking the wrong section of a prerequisite course, a section that did not really prepare us for the higher level courses that followed. Such situations point to the fact that in planning effective instruction, it is extremely important to identify exactly what prerequisite skills, knowledge, and attitudes students must possess before they begin your instruction.

In order to identify the prerequisites your students should possess before you begin teaching them a particular skill, knowledge, or attitude, simply ask yourself, "What do the students have to know or be able to do before I start teaching them?" While this is a fairly straightforward question, it requires some analysis to identify the appropriate skills, knowledge, and attitudes. Too often, we assume that students have the skills they need to begin learning a particular topic.

The concept of prerequisites is perhaps more easily understood in the context of teaching something such as long division. If we assume that the students are ready for instruction on this topic, then they certainly must have the following as a minimum set of prerequisites: the ability to add, subtract, and multiply. If students do not have these skills, then they will have a great deal of difficulty using the procedures that we teach them for doing long division because such procedures will include the use of these skills.

If we can assume that our students already possess the prerequisites we identify, then there is no need to modify our objectives or the instruction that will follow. If, however, we determine that our students do not have the prerequisites, then we must modify our objectives by adding additional skills to our list of those to be taught in order to compensate for the prerequisites the students do not have. If we fail to do so, our instruction will invariably fail. In the second problem scenario, Ms. Helmer has an objective on computing percentages that requires many prerequisite skills that the low-ability students apparently do not have.

When we talk about prerequisites, we are talking about very specific skills that students need to have before they begin our instruction. For now, let us return to our classification of students in terms of above average, average, and below average (as discussed in Chapter 2). How does that affect our consideration of prerequisites? Clearly, those students who are considered gifted have a larger pool of knowledge and skills than those in the lower categories. We can, with greater certainty, assume that they have the prerequisites necessary for the instruction we are to provide. Similarly, if we are dealing with below-average students, we may conclude that they are less likely to have retained the prerequisite skills and knowledge required for beginning instruction on a new skill. In such a situation, while we may not have to modify our objective, it will be critically important to help our students recall the prerequisites as they begin to learn the new information.

Another way in which we must modify our instruction for below-average learners is to accommodate their particular learning strategies. Usually such learners have some difficulty understanding written information and are not good at remembering that information. Therefore, we may need to modify our objectives by breaking them into smaller steps, which can be achieved and retained more easily. In our second problem scenario, before Ms. Helmer taught her students how to solve percentage problems, perhaps she should have reviewed fractions with them and provided them with some real-world applications of percentages. In addition, perhaps the instruction should have been less formal and more interactive in order to stimulate student participation.

Identifying Students' Prerequisite Skills
The assessment of prerequisite skills, knowledge, and attitudes does not continue on a formal basis throughout the academic year because so much of our instruction builds on the preceding instruction. Thus, when we test students following one segment of instruction, the results of the test provide us with information regarding how well students are prepared for the next segment. So, in one sense, when we give a test at the end of one instructional unit, it not only serves as an indication of what the student learned in that unit, but also as an indication of whether the student has the necessary prerequisites to proceed to the next unit. The key issue then becomes whether we provide additional instructional time to those students who have not acquired the necessary prerequisites. Mastery learning is the name given to an instructional approach designed to provide learners with the instructional time they need. This approach is discussed in greater detail in Chapter 7.

Perhaps the most common method for assessing prerequisite skills and knowledge involves administering a pretest to students. This test may have been given at the end of the last school year, but it is more effective if it is given just prior to the beginning of instruction on a particular topic. The content of the test is not what you are going to teach, but rather items that assess the knowledge and skills students should have when you begin instruction.

If some of the prerequisites your students must possess are motor skills or attitudes, then rather than giving them a written test, it is more appropriate to observe the students as they demonstrate some of these prerequisite skills.

In Chapter 6, we will describe how you can go about designing tests to assess prerequisite skills. For the moment, it is important to recognize that knowing where your students are starting from is an important aspect of the instructional planning process and that the results of this analysis may lead to an immediate modification of the goals and objectives in your instructional plan.

PRACTICE

1. Listed below are seven objectives. Read each objective and determine what domain it is in and if it is a complete three-component objective. If not, indicate what is missing and correct the objective.

   A. Given a lathe, the student will operate it by making a round post out of a square block.

   B. Without any aid, identify the major crops raised in the southeastern United States by selecting the four correct items from a list of seven.

    C. The student will choose not to bump into other students who pass him or her in a hallway.

    D. Given fifteen colored blocks, the student will be able to classify them correctly on the basis of their color.

    E. Given a poorly written paragraph, the student will edit it and correct 90 percent of the errors.

    F. The student will know all about photosynthesis.

    G. Without the use of any aids, the student will be able to match at least eight items correctly.

2. Listed below are three possible goals that might be established by a school district. For each goal, list at least one objective.

    A. Be a good citizen.

    B. Be a learner throughout life.

    C. Know the basic skills of arithmetic.

3. Listed below are four objectives. Indicate how, if at all, you would modify these objectives for the following two purposes: first, if you were to inform your students what they were going to learn in your class, and second, if you were to tell parents at an open house what their children were learning in your class.

    A. With the aid of the text, the student can correctly list at least four causes of the Civil War.

    B. Given a standard baseball field, the student can throw from home plate to first base so that the ball can be caught by a person at first base four out of five times.

    C. Given a choice of attending or not attending, the student will choose to go to a symphony concert at least one out of two times.

    D. Given a list of ten vocabulary words, the student will correctly read eight.

4. Listed below are three intellectual skills. Classify these skills as concept learning, rule using, or problem solving.

    A. Students will be able to place commas at appropriate places in a paragraph.

    B. Students will be able to identify verbs in sentences.

    C. Students will be able to edit a poorly written paragraph.

5. Which of the following appear to be appropriate prerequisites for the instructional activities listed?

    A. Draw a straight line before learning to letter.

    B. Add before learning to multiply.

    C. Interpret decimals before learning to compute percents.

    D. Write paragraphs before learning to identify musical instruments.

6. How would you modify your instructional objectives if you found that

    A. your students were quite low in ability?
    B. your students were above average in ability?
    C. your students knew about half the prerequisites for your instruction?
    D. your students fell into two general groups: half of the students knew the prerequisites for your instruction; the other half did not?
    E. your students had poor attitudes about the content that you were about to teach?

7. It is generally not necessary for teachers to assess continually students' prerequisite skills, knowledge, and attitudes for every lesson throughout the year. Why?

8. Mr. Smith is preparing a test on the Civil War but is not sure what should be on his test. As we stated earlier, objectives serve many purposes. How could objectives be helpful to Mr. Smith?

FEEDBACK

1. A. *Psychomotor skill.* This objective is complete because the conditions and the behavior are specified along with a qualitative description of the criterion. However, if the speed with which this task is done is of importance, then a criterion involving time, such as "within fifteen minutes," should have been added to the objective.
   B. *Verbal Information.* This objective clearly specifies a behavior (identify), conditions (without any aid), and standard (selecting the correct four from the list of seven). The objective is properly written.
   C. *Attitude.* This objective, dealing with bumping into students in the hall is complete. While it seems to be rather vague, it reflects the kinds of problems we have when we start writing attitudinal objectives. As an alternative, we could say, "In a crowded hallway, the student will let other students pass by without bumping them." Here the criterion would be "without bumping them" and the condition would be "in a crowded hallway."
   D. *Intellectual Skill.* This is a complete objective. Any time a word like "correctly" appears in an objective, we have to assume that 100 percent correct performance is desired. In this case, unless we wanted the student to classify blocks with 100 percent

accuracy, a criterion such as "twelve out of fifteen" would have to be stated.

E. *Intellectual Skill.* This objective dealing with proofreading a paragraph and finding and correcting the errors is appropriately written.

F. We hope that you found this to be a very unsatisfactory objective. "Knowing all about photosynthesis" is not an acceptable objective for a number of reasons. First of all, we really don't know what the behavior is; we don't know what "knowing" really means. It might mean describing the process or correctly ordering the steps in the process. In addition, it is unclear as to the conditions under which the students would indicate what they know about photosynthesis. It is also unclear as to how well they would have to know it. If we knew all of these things, we would have a much better statement of the objective. The objective might be "Without any aid, the student will describe photosynthesis as the process which plants use to convert the sun's energy into food." In this case, the criterion is an actual description of the words that the student should approximate in his or her answer.

G. We hope you recognized this objective as a form of the "universal objective." It has all three components, but can you tell what the student will really know or be able to do after completing the objective?

2. You were asked to develop objectives for each of the goals that were listed. There is an infinite array of objectives that might have been listed, but let us give you some examples.

A. For the goal "Be a good citizen," you might have stated "Given a situation in which an election of a class officer is to be held, the student will always choose to cast a vote."

B. For the goal "Be a learner throughout life," you might have written an objective such as "Given a situation in which there is no teacher, the student can describe how to go about learning a new topic." Or you might be more specific by saying "Given fifteen minutes in the school library, the student will be able to locate at least two books on a topic that will be assigned to him or her."

C. For the goal "Know the basic skills of arithmetic," you might have an objective such as "Without any aid, the student will be able to solve fifty single-digit addition problems within two minutes." Your objectives might be quite different from the ones we have listed. However, make sure that each contains specific behaviors that could be observed, the conditions under which those behaviors occur, and the standards that can be used to judge whether the behavior is performed in a satisfactory manner.

3. You were presented with four objectives and asked how you would modify those objectives if you were going to communicate them to students and to parents. You might argue that in each case it is important to be very explicit when communicating with students and therefore they are entitled to see the entire objective as it was listed. On the other hand, you might argue that the conditions associated with each of the objectives are not that critical or are implied. For example, in the case of the baseball throwing objective, it might not be necessary to indicate that the behavior will be done on a "standard baseball field."

   What do you think should be said to the parents? In communicating with them, you might drop both the conditions and the criteria. That is, what you want the parents to know is that the students are learning about the Civil War, or learning to throw a baseball, or learning to read vocabulary words, or learning to appreciate symphony music. It may not be necessary to be any more specific with parents than that, unless there is a specific problem with a student. Then more details might be helpful.

4. The three types of intellectual skills are: (a) rules, (b) concepts, and (c) problem solving.

5. For each of the first three situations, namely teaching lettering, multiplication, and percents, the skills that have been indicated are some of the prerequisites students must possess in order for them to acquire the new skills that will be taught to them. However, in our last example it is not necessary to know that students can write paragraphs before teaching them to identify musical instruments. It may be desirable if they know how to write paragraphs, but it is not a logical prerequisite skill to learning to identify musical instruments. It is necessary to be on guard for false prerequisites—skills that sometimes are nice to know but certainly are not required to learn the skills that we are about to teach.

6. A. With a lower ability group, you may find that you have to add additional objectives as prerequisites if the group does not already possess them, and you may also find that you need to break larger objectives down into smaller steps for these particular learners.

   B. With above average students, it is unlikely that you will make any changes in your objectives, unless you determine that your students already possess the skills that you intend to teach them. You would then add additional objectives on more advanced topics.

C. If you found that your students had only half the prerequisites they needed, then the logical thing to do would be to add the prerequisites they do not have to your list of objectives for the lesson. That is, first teach the students those prerequisite skills that they must have in order to learn the skills to be taught in your lesson.

D. The situation in which half the students have the prerequisite skills and the other half do not poses a difficult but common situation for the teacher. One solution is to place the students into two groups based on their prior knowledge and provide different instruction to the two groups. Or, we can teach all of the students the prerequisite skills, knowing that half of them do not need that instruction. There are several ways in which your instructional activities can be modified to accommodate the situation, but the typical solution is to add the prerequisites as objectives for your instruction.

E. If your students had negative attitudes about the content you were about to teach, rather than changing your objectives you might decide to overcome the problem by building some highly motivating activities into your instruction. This approach to overcoming negative attitudes will be discussed in greater detail in Chapter 7.

7. By the middle of the school year, you will be fairly certain about the general ability of the students in your classes, along with their knowledge of the specific prerequisites for the topics for which you will be providing instruction. However, during the early part of the school year or before you begin instruction on an entirely new topic, it is very important that you test students on the prerequisite skills, knowledge, and attitudes required for the new topic.

8. You were asked to describe how Mr. Smith might use objectives to help him prepare a test on the Civil War. We hope that you said that if Mr. Smith had some specific objectives describing the skills or knowledge he wanted his students to acquire about the Civil War, then he could develop a test that reflected the behaviors described in those objectives. For example, if one of his objectives was to have students identify the sites of the major battles of the Civil War, then that would certainly have to be one of the questions on the test. If another of his objectives involved a higher-level problem-solving skill, such as "The student will describe his or her interpretation of the probable consequences

if the South had won the Civil War," then an essay question asking the student to do this should appear on the test. Using instructional objectives to help design tests is a topic we will discuss in greater detail in Chapter 5.

APPLICATION

In the previous chapter, as part of the application activities, you wrote several instructional goals. Now you should write one or more objectives for each of those goals, making sure that you write at least one objective in each of the four domains of learning. Write each objective as though you were going to use it for instructional planning purposes. That is, make sure that it is a three-component objective that describes a specific behavior, conditions, and criteria.

Describe in detail the characteristics of the students who will receive the instruction you are planning. Categorize the students as above average, average, or below average. Indicate the prerequisites for each of your objectives and state how you will determine if the students have them. Indicate how your objectives might have to be modified in light of your analysis of your students.

SUMMARY

In this chapter we have defined objectives as explicit descriptions of what students will be able to do as a result of the instruction they receive. An objective typically consists of three components: the *behavior* expected of the student, the *conditions* under which this behavior will be demonstrated, and the *standard* or *criterion* that must be reached by the student. When objectives are used for planning instruction, all three components should be in place. However, when communicating with parents, students, or the community, it is often beneficial to shorten the objectives to emphasize the behaviors to be learned.

Most objectives can be classified into one of four types, or domains, of learning outcomes: *knowledge, intellectual skills, motor skills,* and *attitudes.* Outcomes in the intellectual skills domain are often further classified as *concept learning, rule using,* or *problem solving.* Being able to distinguish among the various domains will be important when you plan instructional activities to help your students achieve your objectives.

As a teacher, you may frequently be provided with the objectives your students will be expected to acquire. In other cases, however, you will have to derive objectives from the goals you identify. As you do so, try to limit yourself to identifying several meaningful objectives that you would like your students to attain at the end of a lesson or a series of related lessons.

Finally, as you go about identifying your objectives, be sure to consider the characteristics of your students. It is particularly important to consider whether your students possess the prerequisite skills necessary for them to comprehend your instruction. If your students do not possess the necessary prerequisites, then you should modify your objectives so that they include those skills.

Planning Instructional Activities

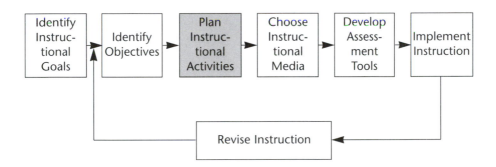

When teachers are planning their instruction, which of the following do you think they spend most of their time thinking about? Goals? Objectives? Tests? Activities?

If you selected *activities,* you were right! Research has shown that most teachers spend the greatest amount of their planning time thinking about and identifying the instructional activities they will use in their classrooms. In this chapter we will describe the types of instructional activities that typically take place during a lesson. We will also describe the factors that you should consider as you go about planning your activities, and we will discuss two procedures you might use to take account of those factors. Finally, we will discuss our ideas regarding the level of detail needed in written lesson plans.

PROBLEM SCENARIO

Mary Gallini was more than disappointed. She had just finished scoring the unit test on writing critical essays. A few of her students had done a good job, but many of them had made a wide variety of errors they simply should not have made. Mary thought back to when she had started planning this unit. There had been so much material to present, and the curriculum guide had not organized it well. So when she had presented the information on writing skills, she felt as if she were jumping all over the place and not staying on track. The students seemed to have liked the games she inserted into several lessons, but that did not seem to have improved their performance. Mary thought "I have got to get organized." Is there anything that Mary could have done to reduce her own frustration, as well as to improve the performance of her students?

CHAPTER OBJECTIVES

The objectives for this chapter are that you will be able to:

1. describe the types of instructional activities that usually take place during a lesson
2. describe the types of instructional activities that should be emphasized when you want students to acquire a particular type of learning outcome
3. describe two different approaches ("objectives-first" and "objectives-second") for planning instructional activities
4. develop a detailed lesson plan that is appropriate for a particular objective and a particular group of students

BACKGROUND INFORMATION

How do teachers go about planning their instructional activities? What factors do they consider as they do so? Research on teacher planning indicates that teachers consider a wide variety of factors, oftentimes considering several of them simultaneously. These factors include:

- the abilities and interests of students,
- the time the teacher has available for an activity,
- the content the teacher is trying to "cover",
- the activity pattern ("routine") the teacher has already established in the class,
- the teacher's repertoire of activities (those types of activities the teacher feels comfortable employing).

These factors are important and should be considered as you plan your instructional activities. But we believe there are at least two other factors you need to consider. These factors are:

- the types of learning outcomes you want your students to attain, and
- the types of instructional activities that will help your students attain those outcomes.

In this chapter, we will focus much of our attention on these two factors.

MAJOR CONCEPTS AND EXAMPLES

Inasmuch as this chapter focuses on instructional activities, we would like to begin by defining that term. When we use the term *instructional activities,* we are referring to the events (or steps) that take place when instruction is presented to students. This definition encompasses those instructional events that involve the active participation of students, as well as those that simply require students to be attentive while some information is being presented to them. Thus, examples of instructional activities include presenting students with information and examples and providing students with practice and feedback.

Another term we would like to define is *instructional method.* When we use the term *instructional method,* we are referring to the general instructional technique used during a lesson or portion of a lesson. Large-group lectures, large-group discussions, and small-group cooperative learning are some examples of the many types of instructional methods used by teachers.

When you talk with teachers and observe what they do in their classrooms, you will find that different teachers favor different methods. Some teachers spend a great deal of class time lecturing; others prefer the use of large-group discussions. Recently, small-group cooperative learning has become a commonly used instructional method. Moreover, there has also been a trend toward student-centered instructional methods. Such methods downplay the role of the teacher as dispenser of information and the student as passive recipient. Instead they focus on actively engaging the student in the learning process.

Regardless of the single method or combination of methods you employ during a lesson, we believe (and research has suggested) that your lesson will be more effective if you incorporate particular types of instructional activities into it. These activities include:

- motivating students
- informing students of objectives
- helping students recall prerequisites
- presenting information and examples
- providing practice and feedback
- summarizing the lesson

Each of these types of activities is described below.

Types of Instructional Activities

Motivating Students

It is not surprising that research indicates that unless you have the attention of your students, it is very hard to get them to learn. In preparing instruction, however, we sometimes overlook this notion. In such instances, we assume that students are motivated and that we do not have to do anything to gain their attention and maintain that attention throughout instruction. At times, however, this assumption is incorrect; we must plan activities that will motivate our students.

Motivating learners is probably one of the most important issues for the teacher in the classroom. How can you get a "hook" into students in order to maintain their attention? There are many strategies you can use to do so. These include:

- Arousing students' curiosity (by presenting them with interesting pictures, displaying unusual phenomena, etc.)
- Making instruction relevant to students' interests (by relating instruction to events going on in the students' lives or to events and personalities that have captured the students' attention)
- Entertaining students (by such techniques as incorporating humor into your lessons, using gamelike activities, setting up simulated versions of real-life events, etc.)
- Getting students to be involved actively in the lesson (by such techniques as asking lots of questions, requiring the students to solve problems, having students participate in small group discussions and other small group activities, etc.)
- Arranging conditions for student success (by asking questions and presenting problems that are at the right level of difficulty for your students. That is, problems and questions should neither be so difficult that most students will be unable to answer them, nor should they be so simple that most students will be bored by them.)
- Being enthusiastic (whether you are lecturing to students or responding to their questions or comments, if you do it with enthusiasm, that enthusiasm is likely to be contagious! In other words, your students are likely to become enthusiastic too.)
- Providing students with rewards that may be tangible (tokens, snacks, etc.), or intangible (praise, a pat on the back, etc.).

Informing Students of Objectives

At a fairly early stage, learners should be informed of what it is that they are going to be able to do when they finish the instructional process. By knowing what will be expected of them, learners may be better able to guide themselves through that process. Indeed, research has shown that in many cases learner performance will be improved if we simply make our objectives explicit before we begin our instruction.

As was discussed in Chapter 3, there are many ways in which we can inform students about our objectives. It is unlikely that you would give them a list of three-component objectives. There may be times when it will not even be necessary to provide anything in writing to students. Simply describing the outcomes of instruction may be sufficient, or you may want to provide examples of what the students will be able to do. Clearly, this second instructional event can be closely related to how to motivate learners if, in fact, they are eager to acquire the skill or knowledge that is to be taught.

Helping Students Recall Prerequisites

We have already defined prerequisites as the skills, knowledge, and attitudes students must have in order to comprehend your instruction. Research has indicated that learning is most effective when we can relate new knowledge and skills to knowledge and skills that we have already learned. In other words, new learning is accomplished by building upon what we already know. If students have already learned the necessary prerequisite skills and knowledge, and they are reminded of them, then the learning of the new task is a relatively straightforward matter. That is why it is important that you help students recall the necessary prerequisites before you begin to teach them some new skills or knowledge.

How can you help students go about recalling prerequisites? You can simply remind students of the necessary prerequisite knowledge and skills (e.g., "now, we already know that the rule for determining the area of a rectangle is . . ."). However, it is often best to ask students to recall the prerequisite knowledge (e.g., "who remembers the rule for determining the area of a rectangle?") and to demonstrate the prerequisite skills ("now, each of you use the rule to determine the area of this rectangle . . .").

If students are unable to recall, or have not learned, the necessary prerequisites, it will be very difficult for them to acquire the new knowledge or skill. Thus, if you find that most of your students lack the prerequisites, then you should teach (or reteach) those prerequisites to your class before attempting to teach them the new skills or knowledge. If only a few students lack the prerequisites, you should try to provide them with special instruction so that they, like the rest of their classmates, will be ready for the new instruction.

Presenting Information and Examples

For most objectives, there is some information that must be presented to the learners, or information that the learners must discover, before they can perform the behavior described in the objective. For example, before most students are able to solve a particular class of problems, such as division problems involving two fractions, they typically are informed of the rule or rules that can be used to solve such problems. Or, if students are learning to analyze the conditions that led to the economic depression in the United States in the 1930s, we must inform them what those conditions were. Similarly, in the case of knowledge objectives, it is obvious that before learners can recall some information, that information must be provided to them. In the case of motor skills, it is necessary to provide learners with a verbal or visual description of the physical process involved in performing a particular skill.

As the examples in the previous paragraph clearly indicate, an important part of the instructional process involves presenting students with the necessary information or arranging conditions so that students are able to discover that information for themselves. Yet, in many lessons, learners are never provided (or given adequate opportunity to discover) the information they need to know. As a teacher, it is important that you plan to present that information to your students or that you help guide students to that information, directing and correcting them as necessary.

In addition to providing learners with the necessary information, it is important to give them examples so that they can see how they can use the information. For example, if we provide learners with the rule for solving division problems involving two fractions, it is important that we demonstrate how to solve such problems. Similarly, it is very important to demonstrate motor skills to learners, regardless of whether we provide them with a description of the steps involved in the performance.

Providing Practice and Feedback

In most cases, in order for students to be able to acquire a particular skill, knowledge, or attitude, they must practice that behavior. Therefore, practice activities should be directly related to the skills, knowledge, and attitudes reflected in your objectives. So, for example, if one of your objectives calls for students to be able to write similes, then the most appropriate practice exercise would be to have your students do just that. Your practice activity for this objective would be insufficient if it were limited to the practice of related behaviors, such as identifying similes in given sentences.

After learners have practiced a behavior, it is important for them to receive some feedback. Feedback is the information a learner receives regarding the answer or answers he or she provided. At a minimum, feedback lets the learner know whether an answer was correct. In addition, feedback may indicate what the correct answer was, why it was correct, and, perhaps, what was wrong with the learner's incorrect answer.

Research indicates that providing learners with feedback is a crucial part of the instructional process. Simply having students practice an activity without providing them with any feedback does not necessarily result in effective learning. Indeed, if a student practices the wrong behaviors and is not corrected, that practice activity is likely to be very counterproductive. Thus, when you are developing your instructional plan, you should think about the type of feedback you will provide to students after they complete your practice activities.

Summarizing the Lesson

It is usually a good idea to end a lesson with some type of summary to bring closure to the lesson and to help reinforce the skills and knowledge your students should have acquired. Oftentimes, it is a good idea to begin the summary by restating, in simple terms, the lesson objective so that students are reminded of the purpose of the lesson. The rest of the summary may simply involve a brief review of the skills that were taught during the lesson. Or you may choose to have the students play a more active role in summarizing the lesson. This may be done by using such techniques as having them summarize what they learned or having them apply what they learned in order to solve a final problem or question that you pose.

Instructional Activities and the Domains of Learning

As we stated at the outset of this chapter, when you are deciding upon the instructional activities that will occur during a lesson, one of the important factors to consider is the type of learning outcome you want your learners to acquire as a result of the lesson. In Chapter 3 we described four domains of learning: knowledge, intellectual skills, motor skills, and attitudes. The six instructional activities we have described are applicable to all four domains. However, research has shown that in order to promote effective learning in the various domains, particular activities should be emphasized during your instruction. These activities vary with the domain of learning.

Knowledge Objectives

With knowledge objectives, the way in which you present new information (i.e., the facts you want your students to recall) is very important. When you are presenting new facts, you should try to present those facts in a context that is meaningful to your students. For example, if your students have already identified where the states are on the map, it may be easier for them to insert the state capitals, as opposed to simply trying to learn the state capitals by memory.

With knowledge objectives, it is also important that you provide your students with extensive practice and feedback. That practice usually consists of writing or verbalizing the knowledge and using it in various ways. Feedback for knowledge objectives usually can consist of simply informing the student of the correct answer or having the student look up the answer. For example, if some students forget the capital of Georgia, they can easily find that information in their instructional materials.

Intellectual-skills Objectives

When we look at the domain of intellectual skills, a number of things become apparent. First, if students do not have the prerequisites necessary to begin instruction on an intellectual-skills objective, it is almost certain that they will be unable to attain that objective. For example, if students do not know how to multiply and subtract, they will be unable to solve long-division problems. Therefore, the establishment of those prerequisites is critical to the success of the instruction.

The use of examples is also very important when you are teaching intellectual skills. In most cases, it will not be sufficient to simply present a set of rules to your students. In addition, you will have to demonstrate the application of those rules so that your students really begin to understand how the rules are to be applied. For example, if you were teaching students how to compute their net worth, you would not only provide the formula, you would also give a number of examples that take different factors into consideration. Some of the factors may not be relevant to net worth. Therefore, using a variety of examples and non-examples (examples that typify mistakes often made in the application of the rules) is extremely important for the acquisition of intellectual skills.

When you are teaching intellectual skills to your students, you should also provide them with sufficient practice and feedback. The use of response-specific feedback is particularly important. Consider a situation in which a student is asked to add $1/3 + 1/3$ and responds that the answer is $2/6$. In this case, it most likely would not be sufficient to inform the student that the correct answer is $2/3$. Instead, it is important that the student is provided with feedback that is specific to the error. In our example, the student would be told that when two fractions with the same denominator are added together, you do not add the two denominators; instead you simply add the numerators and place the total over the denominator that appeared in both fractions.

Motor Skills

Before students can properly perform a motor skill, they must know the "executive routine," or series of steps, that must be followed in the process of performing that skill. Moreover, as you are describing this series of steps to your students, it is important to demonstrate those steps for them. In other words, informing students of the necessary information (i.e., the series of steps) and providing them with examples are crucial when you are teaching motor skills.

After students have learned the executive routine for a motor skill, then practice and feedback become critical. In many situations, the students might begin by practicing the components that make up the skill and then practice integrating those components into a smooth motor performance. As for feedback, with some motor skills the execution of the act itself provides sufficient feedback to indicate to students whether they performed the skill correctly. Archery is an example. However, in other situations like swimming, students must be observed by the teacher, who can tell them what is right or wrong.

Attitude Objectives

In developing an instructional plan for an attitude, two instructional activities are extremely important. The first activity is motivation. Determining ways in which to gain or maintain students' attention in the instruction, while always important, is particularly critical when you are working on attitude objectives. It is unlikely that we will be able to have our learners acquire new attitudes if we cannot motivate them to pay attention to the message we are trying to present.

When it comes to teaching attitudes, a second important instructional activity is providing students with information about, and examples of, the attitudinal choices we would like them to make. Research has shown that this instructional activity is most likely to be effective if someone whom your students admire demonstrates (or verbally promotes) the behavior you want your students to acquire. We often see this technique employed in television commercials in which the advertiser attempts to influence our thinking by having people we admire advocate the use of certain products or advocate not participating in certain kinds of activities.

The following chart summarizes our discussion of the types of instructional activities that are most important when you are trying to have your learners acquire a particular type of learning outcome.

Critical Instructional Activities by Learning Domain

Domain	Critical Activities
Knowledge	Presenting information (in a meaningful context) Providing practice and feedback
Intellectual skills	Helping students recall prerequisites Presenting examples (and non-examples) Providing practice and feedback (especially response-specific feedback)
Motor skills	Presenting information (the "executive routine") Presenting examples (executing the skill) Providing practice and feedback
Attitudes	Motivating students Presenting information and examples (by someone students admire)

Although certain types of instructional events should be emphasized depending upon the type of learning outcome you are focusing upon, that does not mean you should exclude the other types of instructional events from your lessons. To the contrary, we believe that each time you are planning a lesson, you should consider incorporating each of the six types of instructional activities we have identified. Of course, upon such consideration you may choose not to include a particular type of event. For example, in some instances, perhaps due to the nature of the instructional content or the consequences of not acquiring a particular skill, learners may be highly motivated before a lesson begins. In such cases, you may decide not to incorporate any motivational activities into your lesson. Or, in other instances, there may be no prerequisite skills or knowledge that your learners will need to recall, thus obviating the need to include that type of instructional event. However, we believe that cases such as these are the exception, rather than the rule. Thus, we believe that all six types of instructional activities should be incorporated into most lesson plans.

Sequencing Instructional Activities

In what sequence should the six types of instructional activities occur? Oftentimes, they occur in the order in which we have described them. However, in many cases you may find yourself using the same type of activity at several different points in a lesson. For example, in order to maintain your students' attention, it's a good idea to incorporate motivational activities at several points in your lesson, not just at the outset. Similarly, in some situations, teachers will present information and examples, and provide practice and feedback at several different points within the same lesson.

There are other common exceptions to the sequence of activities that we have proposed. For example, some teachers begin a lesson by reviewing some prerequisite skills. This activity may be followed by informing the students of the lesson objectives and then engaging the students in some motivational activity. In other cases, such as those where students are expected to derive (or "discover") the rules necessary to solve a problem, teachers begin the lesson by presenting students with practice activities. Moreover, there are many cases where a single classroom event incorporates two or more of the types of instructional activities we have described. For example, teachers may have students participate in a game that is motivational, presents information to the students, and also provides them with practice and feedback.

Other Types of Instructional Activities

In addition to the six types of instructional activities described above, which we believe you should incorporate into most of your lessons, there are two other types of instructional activities that may be employed on a less frequent basis. These types of activities are providing enrichment and providing remediation. Enrichment activities are intended to extend student knowledge or skills beyond that required. In contrast, remedial activities are designed to enable students to attain an objective they were unable to attain previously.

Why are enrichment and remedial activities necessary? While we would like to think that at the conclusion of a lesson all of our students will achieve the behaviors that our lesson is designed to teach, this outcome is quite unlikely. There is a much greater likelihood that, at least initially, some of our learners will acquire the behaviors and others will not. Therefore, if we want all our students to master an objective, we must be prepared to provide remedial activities for the unsuccessful learners and enrichment activities for those who are successful. The remedial activities should be directly targeted on the problems demonstrated by the students in the original instruction. The enrichment activities should enable students to take what they have already learned and apply it in new and interesting situations. These enrichment activities certainly should not be viewed as punitive, but rather as opportunities for students who are successful to go on to other topics or do other things that are important to them.

Instructional Activities for Different Types of Students

It is interesting to examine instructional activities with regard to the different types of learners that we have discussed in previous chapters. How does an instructional plan vary for below-average, average, and above-average students? In the case of below-average learners, we have indicated that often we have to break objectives down into smaller objectives to have the instruction more nearly fit their ability to learn in the classroom. In addition, as we look at various instructional activities we can see that with below-average learners, it is even more important to increase your emphasis on motivation and make sure that the learners have the necessary prerequisite knowledge. Furthermore, a common observation of those who teach these students is that they often forget the knowledge that they have seemingly acquired. Therefore, prior to new instruction, such students frequently must be reminded of what they have already learned.

In working with below-average learners, it also is important to use a large number of examples, giving a lot of practice and feedback in which they experience success. Finally, with below-average learners it is particularly important to plan for remedial activities. If, through the use of remedial activities, you can ensure that your students attain one set of objectives before you proceed with instruction on the next set, then it will be less likely that your learners will experience "cumulative failure"—the building of failure upon failure that often occurs with below-average learners.

In contrast to the approach taken with below-average learners, it is often possible with above-average students actually to omit some of the activities in an instructional plan. For example, you may find that these learners are extremely motivated to learn the objectives and therefore no special effort to motivate them is necessary. There also may be little concern with informing them of the prerequisites because we are certain they already have them. Also, because of the ability of these students to grasp ideas rapidly, the number of examples and non-examples you present may be reduced, as may the amount of practice and feedback you provide. Therefore, in developing a strategy for above-average students, it is important to recognize the abilities and knowledge that they bring to the learning situation and not create inefficient instruction that bores them.

When we consider average learners, the events of instruction seem to be made for them. With such learners, the emphasis we place upon each instructional event is likely to be influenced much more heavily by the type of learning outcome we are working with, rather than the type of learner. After we have tried out our instructional plan with our students, regardless of their special characteristics, we may choose to modify it. How to decide upon such modifications will be discussed in Chapter 8.

Strategies for Planning Your Instructional Activities

Teachers often begin planning their lessons by thinking about factors such as those we identified at the outset of this chapter. For example, a teacher may begin by thinking about the abilities and interests of her students, the content she is trying to cover, and the instructional time she has available. Or a teacher may begin by thinking about a particular type of activity he knows his students enjoy (e.g., participating in a "quiz show") and then thinking about how he might relate that activity to the content he is trying to cover. We would like to suggest that you use a different strategy.

The "Objectives-first" Approach

We suggest that when you start thinking about the instructional activities you will use during a lesson, you should begin by thinking about the objective for that lesson and the type of learning outcome it represents. Then plan your instructional activities so as to help your students attain that objective, paying particular attention to the types of activities that are critical to its attainment. Let's look at an example of how you might use this strategy.

Suppose that you are a seventh-grade mathematics teacher planning a lesson intended to teach students how to solve written word problems that involve rate, time, and distance. How will you go about planning the instructional activities that will comprise this lesson?

Under the "objectives-first" approach, you would begin by translating your goal into a specific objective, such as, "The student will correctly solve written word problems involving rate, time, and distance by using the formula $D = R \times T$." You would then identify the type of learning outcome this objective represents and the types of instructional activities that are critical for its attainment. Because the objective represents an intellectual skill, the critical instructional activities you will need to focus on are helping students recall the necessary prerequisite skills, presenting students with a variety of examples of how to perform the skill and providing the students with lots of practice and response-specific feedback. We will assume that this instruction is being prepared for average seventh graders, so there will be no special variations in the instructional plan to accommodate the characteristics of these students. With this information in mind, you might develop the set of instructional activities described in Table 4.1. Please note that this table represents a highly detailed lesson plan. In the next section of this chapter we will discuss written lesson plans and how detailed they should be.

It should be noted that the instructional plan presented in Table 4.1 is just one of many possible plans for teaching a procedure for solving mathematical word problems. In addition, please note that there are still a number of decisions to be made with regard to the strategy. For example, we must decide upon what media will be incorporated into the presentation of the instruction. We also have to develop the actual worksheets we will use, and we must determine the roles the teacher and the textbook will play with regard to this topic. Exact classroom procedures will also have to be worked out, although a number of them are suggested in the activities.

Perhaps the most important thing to note about this plan is that we developed it by first having a clear picture of what our objective was. We then planned our activities to help students attain that objective. We hope you will use the same general strategy as you go about planning your instructional activities.

Turning to the problem scenario presented at the beginning of this chapter, if Ms. Gallini had begun planning her lessons by clearly identifying the objectives she wanted her students to acquire, it is likely she would have planned a sequence of instructional activities that were more effective, that is, that would have resulted in a greater percentage of her students attaining her objectives. However, experience tells us that most teachers do not follow this "objectives-first" strategy; instead they plan their instructional activities without giving much, if any, forethought to their objectives. This leads us to another suggestion regarding the planning of instructional activities.

TABLE 4.1: Example of a Highly Detailed Lesson Plan

1. *Motivation.* Remind students that the speed limits on the highways in our state have recently increased. If we take a trip elsewhere in our state (to relatives, friends, recreation areas, for example) it will take less time to get there if we travel at the speed limit. How can we figure out how much time it will take?
2. *Objective.* Tell the students that the objective is to be able to solve problems in which they have to figure how far, how fast, or how long it will take to travel, given written information about two of these factors. They will use a mathematical formula to do this.
3. *Prerequisites.* We know that the students have the basic math skills (add, subtract, multiply, and divide), that they comprehend the concept of travel and movement from one point to another, and we remind them that they know that movement requires time. Perhaps the most critical prerequisite is understanding how a formula like $D = R \times T$ is used to determine an unknown component within that formula. Perhaps reviewing a similar formula that the students have already used would be appropriate.
4. *Information and Examples.* Distance = Rate × Time ($D = R \times T$). Explain each concept: rate, time, and distance. Provide numerous examples, first using the easiest situation in which rate and time are multiplied in order to determine distance. Then move to examples in which rate equals distance divided by time, and time equals distance divided by rate. Present each example in the context of a word problem involving (a) traveling in a car, train, plane, or boat, or (b) running or walking.
5. *Practice and Feedback.* Provide students with a set of ten problems that vary in terms of whether the students have to solve for time, rate, or distance. For variety in instructional approach and in order to have the students help each other, organize the students into teams and give them thirty minutes to solve the problems. Afterwards, review the problems in detail with the entire class and explain the correct answers. If overall performance is poor, review the information with new examples and give additional practice problems for students to work on individually. With this approach, it will be possible to identify exactly which students are still having problems.
6. Remind students that today we have learned to solve word problems involving rate, time, and distance. Ask them to state the formula they would use to solve each type of problem covered during the lesson.

The "Objectives-second" Approach

If you find yourself planning your instructional activities without thinking about your objectives first, then we suggest that you think about your objectives second! What we mean is, after you have thought of an activity you would like to include in a lesson, ask yourself this question:

> Will this activity help my students attain any objective(s)
> I want them to acquire?

If you are unable to answer this question in the affirmative, that doesn't mean that you should throw out your plans for that activity. We believe that there is always room for some instructional activities that are not directly in support of an objective. However, if you find that a great deal of the activities you are planning fall into this category, then we urge you to spend some more time planning activities using the "objectives-first" approach!

Describing Your Instructional Activities in Writing: The Lesson Plan

Regardless of how you go about planning your instructional activities, as you do so it is a good idea to record some of your plans in writing. How detailed should these plans be? If you are a novice teacher, we recommend that your written plans be rather detailed. Why do we feel this way?

As we indicated in Chapter 1, experienced teachers can draw upon their rich set of teaching experiences to form elaborate mental images of a lesson. Thus, their written plans are often quite sketchy. In contrast, if you are a novice teacher, you do not have a rich set of teaching experiences to draw upon. However, we believe that if you take the time to think about and develop detailed written plans, it is likely that you will start to conceive of some instructional possibilities that you would not have thought of otherwise. And in doing so, you will establish a firm planning base that will enable you to develop less detailed written plans as you gain more teaching experience.

Our earlier description of the lesson on rate, time, and distance is an example of a highly detailed lesson plan. If you were simply preparing a lesson plan for your own use, it is unlikely that you would prepare one that was so detailed. However, when we are working in a teacher education program with students who have had little or no experience in preparing lessons, we like to have them prepare plans that are as detailed as our example. The reason we ask them to do so is that without such detail, it is difficult for us to provide them with the feedback they need to improve the quality of their instructional planning. If your instructor asks you to develop detailed plans like the example we have provided, he or she is most likely doing so for the very same reason. We hope you will remember this and not be discouraged or put off by the amount of detail you are asked to provide.

What do less detailed lesson plans look like? The variety of formats you can use to describe your lesson is limitless. What follow are but three examples of the same lesson plan, each presented in a different format. As you will see, in two instances, the lesson plan is described in some detail, whereas in the third the description is quite sketchy.

TABLE 4.2:   Moderately Detailed Lesson Plan—First Example

Objective: The student will correctly solve written word problems involving rate, time, and distance by using the formula $D = R \times T$

Type of Instructional Activity	Teacher's Role	Students' Role	Role of Other Media
1. Motivation	a. remind students of increase in state speed limits b. ask students: how can we figure out how long will it take to get to various places?	c. respond to various questions	
2. Objective	a. tell students they will solve word problems involving how far, fast, and long it takes to travel		
3. Prerequisites	a. remind students that travel takes time b. remind students how to use an algebraic equation (e.g., $A = L \times W$)		
4. Information and examples	a. explain concepts of rate, time, distance b. explain formula $D = R \times T$ c. give examples using each part of the formula as the unknown; use "real world" contexts (plane, train, etc.)		
5. Practice and feedback	a. group students to work on set of 10 written problems c. review answers to problems with class	b. work in small groups to solve problems	
6. Additional examples	a. if needed, provide additional examples		
7. Additional practice and feedback	a. if needed, give students additional problems to work on individually c. review answers to problems with class	b. work on problems	
8. Summary	a. Remind students: we have learned how to solve word problems involving rate, time, and distance. b. Ask students to state the formula for each type of problem covered	c. respond to questions	

Examples of Moderately Detailed Lesson Plans

As you are preparing your lesson plan, we recommend that you describe each instructional activity in terms of:

- your role (what you will say and do)
- your students' role (what students will do), and
- how other media, if any, are to be employed (the next chapter will deal with this issue).

The lesson plan format shown in Table 4.2 specifically calls for all three pieces of information.

Table 4.3 provides another example of a moderately detailed lesson plan. Although the amount of information contained in the lesson plan is the same as that contained in the previous example, the format that is used is a simpler one.

TABLE 4.3: Moderately Detailed Lesson Plan—Second Example

Objective: The student will correctly solve written word problems involving rate, time, and distance by using the formula $D = R \times T$

Type of Instructional Activity	Description
1. Motivation	a. remind students of increase in state speed limits b. ask students: how can we figure out how long will it take to get to various places?
2. Objective	a. tell students they will solve word problems involving how far, fast, and long it takes to travel
3. Prerequisites	a. remind students that travel takes time b. remind students how to use an algebraic equation (e.g., $A = L \times W$)
4. Information and examples	a. explain concepts of rate, time, distance b. explain formula $D = R \times T$ c. give examples of using each part of the formula as the unknown; use "real world" contexts (plane, train, etc.)
5. Practice and feedback	a. group students to work on set of 10 written problems b. review answers to problems with class
6. Additional examples	a. if needed, provide additional examples
7. Additional practice and feedback	a. if needed, give students additional problems to work on individually b. review answers to problems with class
8. Summary	a. Remind students: we have learned how to solve word problems involving rate, time, and distance. b. Ask students to state the formula for each type of problem covered.

Example of a Sketchy Lesson Plan
We have noticed that there is a great deal of variation in the amount of detail experienced teachers include in their written lesson plans. Some experienced teachers will develop written plans that are about as detailed as the previous example, but many others often rely much more heavily on mental planning, recalling and employing specific activities that previously worked in similar or identical instructional situations. These teachers often develop very sketchy written plans. What follows is an example of such a plan. If you are a novice teacher preparing plans as detailed as the first example we presented in this chapter, you may take heart in the fact that the lesson planning experiences you are gaining now should eventually enable you to plan and deliver very effective instruction, even though the written plans you prepare may be as sketchy (or sketchier!) than the one presented below.

Sketchy Lesson Plan

- Discuss new state speed limits
- State objective
- Review use of algebraic formulas (e.g., A = L × W)
- Present D = R × T
- Group and individual practice
- Summary

PRACTICE

1. Listed below are the key words for the six instructional activities included in an instructional plan. Indicate your understanding of these events by briefly describing each one.

   A. Motivation of students
   B. Objectives
   C. Prerequisites
   D. Information and Examples
   E. Practice and Feedback
   F. Summary

2. Listed below are the four major domains of instructional goals and learning outcomes for students. After each goal, list the instructional events that would receive special consideration if you were teaching an objective in that domain.

   A. Knowledge
   B. Intellectual Skills
   C. Motor Skills
   D. Attitude

3. Identify a topic area that you might have to teach in the future. Describe how you would use the "objectives-first" approach to identify the critical activities to include in the instruction.
4. Assume that a colleague has identified "a great activity" to use in class. Describe how you might use the "objectives-second" approach to determine if this really is a great activity.
5. Listed below are some typical comments that might be heard from students during or after studying a particular topic. Based upon each comment, decide which instructional activity may have been missing from the instructional plan used by the teacher. For example, if a student said "I studied and studied, but I never really understood what it was I was supposed to be learning," we would imagine that the student did not understand what the objective of the lesson was. Apparently, the teacher had not made the objective clear to the student. Now, look at each of the comments below, and decide what instructional activity may have been missing.

   A. "I turned in my answers to the homework problems he gave us, but I never found out how well I did."
   B. "I have no idea why we are studying this topic. It doesn't seem to have anything to do with anything I'm interested in."
   C. "We've moved on to unit three and I still don't understand the stuff from unit two!"
   D. "We spent a lot of time working on some activities, but I was never clear about exactly what the formula was that we were supposed to be applying. If he had just shown us how to use the formula, maybe I could have done better."
   E. "We go from lecture to lecture, but I never got a chance to try to use the skills the teacher is teaching. . . ."
   F. "I listened as closely as I could to what the teacher said in class, but I didn't understand what she was talking about. I seem to be missing something that I should know to understand this topic."
   G. "I didn't like this lesson because I never understood its purpose."

6. Listed below is a goal and an objective, which is intended for all fourth-grade students—below average, average and above average. Develop an instructional plan for achieving this objective by indicating what you would do for each of the six major instructional activities.
   Goal: Practice safety habits at home and school.
   Objective: Students choose to practice safe bicycle riding at all times.

You may find this a little difficult, but it brings out some important points, so go ahead and give it a try.

FEEDBACK

1. Check the appropriate section of this chapter for the answers to this question.
2. Check the table titled Critical Instructional Activities by Learning Domain for the answers to this question.
3. In the "objectives-first" approach you identify exactly what it is that learners will be able to do when they finish your instruction; *then* you select or develop activities that help the learners achieve these objectives.
4. In the "objectives-second" approach you would ask your colleague to identify the objective that will be achieved by having students participate in the proposed activity. If the activity doesn't seem to support any objective, then, quite possibly it isn't so great (or the teacher should develop a new objective—that is always a possibility.)
5. Activities that were probably omitted from the instructional plan:

   A. Feedback for the practice
   B. Motivation
   C. Remediation or prerequisites
   D. Information and examples
   E. Practice and feedback
   F. Prerequisites
   G. Objectives

6. This is an interesting objective for a number of reasons. First of all, we hope you recognized that it is in the attitudinal domain and therefore we will be particularly concerned about the motivation of the students and the way in which we present the information to them. Secondly, the plan must apply to all fourth graders, below average, average, and above average. It is not clear whether these ability levels are relevant to the teaching of an attitude since they are based primarily upon the students' intellectual skills, not their attitudes. The instructional plan described below was developed with these thoughts in mind. Of course, the activities we propose are just one of many possible sets for teaching this objective. The plan you developed may be quite different, but still may be very appropriate.

   A. *Motivation.* While it may be possible to point out the seriousness of injuries due to careless bicycle riding habits, there probably are more positive ways to show the benefits of safe riding. Having the fourth graders organize a schoolwide campaign to promote safe riding might be a good source of motivation.
   B. *Objectives.* We would indicate to the students that we want them

to choose to ride their bicycles safely in a variety of riding situations. They might be provided pictures of such situations.

C. *Prerequisites.* Can we assume that all fourth graders have bicycles and can ride a bike? This poses a problem, as does getting the students to bring their bicycles to school. Those who ride the bus will obviously have difficulties. Therefore, this objective might come later in the year and have as its prerequisite that the students are able to ride a bicycle. Students who do not know how may be taught this skill in their physical education class.

D. *Information and Examples.* Select a role model admired by the students, such as a well-known older student or someone from the community. Have this person come in and talk to the students and demonstrate the rules for safely riding a bicycle. An important aspect of this event is to point out the major rules and describe instances in which those rules would be important.

E. *Practice and Feedback.* Give students the opportunity to ride the bicycles on the school grounds in situations that simulate problems they might encounter riding to and from school. Teachers and fellow students will provide the children with feedback regarding unsafe practices.

F. *Summary.* After the students have practiced riding safely, they could be reminded about the importance of their decisions when they are riding their bicycles at any time. Perhaps critical comments made by the role model during the instruction could be reviewed and students asked to describe how they will ride safely in the future.

APPLICATION

Choose two of the objectives you have written. Make sure they are from two different learning domains. For each objective, develop a lesson plan in the format shown in Table 4.1. Be able to explain your rationale for each of the instructional activities in your plan.

SUMMARY

In this chapter, we have indicated that instructional activities are the events or steps that take place when instruction is presented to students. This definition includes those events that involve active student participation as well as those events that simply require students to be attentive.

We have described six types of instructional activities that should occur during most lessons. These six are:

- Motivating students
- Informing students of objectives
- Helping students recall prerequisites
- Presenting information and examples
- Providing practice and feedback
- Summarizing the lesson

In addition to these six, there are two other types of activities that we believe are important but which can be employed on a less frequent basis: providing enrichment and remediation for students.

Depending on the type of learning outcome you want your students to attain, certain instructional activities should be emphasized during a lesson. For example, if you would like your students to acquire a particular attitudinal objective, it is particularly useful to motivate the students and have someone they respect present them with the necessary information and examples. Certain types of activities may also be emphasized or omitted based on the characteristics of your students.

How should you go about planning your instructional activities? We have suggested two different approaches. Under the "objectives-first" approach, you begin by thinking about your lesson objective and the type of learning outcome it represents and then planning instructional activities that will help students attain that outcome. Under the "objectives-second" approach, you begin by planning instructional activities and then examining whether those activities will help students acquire any objectives you would like them to attain.

Finally, we have indicated that the instructional planning skills of novice teachers are likely to be improved if the teachers develop fairly detailed written lesson plans. However, as novice teachers gain more experience, the need for detailed written plans will diminish.

C H A P T E R 5

Choosing
Instructional Media

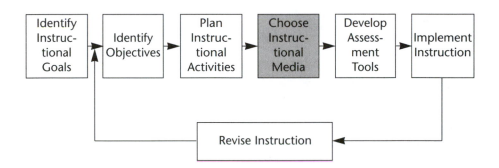

In the previous chapter, we indicated that as you are preparing your lesson plan, you should describe each instructional activity in terms of your role, your students' role, and the role that will be played by other instructional media. In some cases, it is quite likely that your instructional activities will be limited to the "traditional" media employed by teachers, namely the chalkboard, textbooks, workbooks, and other supplementary print materials. However, there are likely to be instances when you will want to use other instructional media as part of your instructional plan. How will you decide whether a particular medium is appropriate? That is the question we will focus upon in this chapter.

PROBLEM SCENARIO

Ms. Washington, a fifth-grade teacher, has just received a brochure about a new computer software program entitled "Capital Ideas." According to the brochure, "'Capital Ideas' is a drill-and-practice program that will make learning the names of state capitals fun! Students are given the names of states and are asked to name the capitals of each one. Each time a student answers correctly, a state flag appears on the dome of a state capitol. After ten correct responses, a simulated fireworks display appears above the dome."

Ms. Washington's students are supposed to learn the names of the state capitals. She wonders whether she should use "Capital Ideas" to help them.

CHAPTER OBJECTIVES

The objectives for this chapter are that you will be able to

1. identify the questions you should ask when choosing an instructional medium
2. indicate whether specific media are appropriate for use in a given instructional situation, and provide a rationale for your answer

BACKGROUND INFORMATION

When you hear or read the term *instructional media,* what do you think of? Many people would say that they think of such things as films, or filmstrips, or overhead projectors. Others, particularly those who have recently been in school settings, are more likely to mention computers. All of these things are examples of instructional media.

We would like to define instructional media as the physical means by which instruction is delivered to students. Thus, our definition of media includes all of the traditional means of delivering instruction (including teachers, chalkboards, textbooks, and other print materials), as well as the newer instructional media, such as computers, CD-ROM, interactive video, and multimedia systems. In this chapter we will be focusing our attention on these newer, less traditional instructional media.

MAJOR CONCEPTS AND EXAMPLES

The instructional media we will be discussing in this chapter are less traditional in the sense that teachers, chalkboard, textbooks, and supplementary print materials are used more frequently as a means of presenting instructional activities to students. Indeed, it is likely that when you choose a means for presenting an instructional activity, you will assume that you will present the activity yourself or that you will use a textbook or supplementary print material to do so. However, there are likely to be instances when you may want to incorporate a different medium in your instructional plan. Under such circumstances, we suggest you ask yourself these three questions: Is the instructional medium you are considering:

1. practical?
2. appropriate in light of your students' characteristics?
3. a good means of presenting a particular instructional activity?

Practicality

The question of whether a medium is practical must be examined in terms of the mediated materials (software) you want to use and the media equipment (hardware) that will be required. It is important to distinguish between media hardware and media software. Media hardware refers to equipment, such as computers, televisions, and tape players. Media software, or mediated materials, are the instructional materials that are presented by means of a piece of media hardware. Examples of mediated materials are computer disks, videocassettes, and audiotapes.

When it comes to software, do not be surprised if the school you work in does not have many of the computer software packages, instructional videotapes, and other mediated materials of which you may be aware. If they are not readily available, what will be the time and cost involved in obtaining or producing them, and are the administrators at your school likely to approve of the expense?

Even if the desired mediated materials are easily obtainable, there are a number of practical questions pertaining to media hardware that you should consider. These include the following:

- Is the necessary media hardware (equipment) readily available to you?
- If the hardware is available, can that hardware be easily used in the instructional environment in which you are working?
- If the necessary hardware is not readily available, what will be the time and cost involved in obtaining it, and will the school administrators approve of the expense?

Student Characteristics

When you are thinking about using an instructional medium, it is important for you also to consider whether that medium is appropriate in light of the characteristics of your students. One factor you should take into consideration is the attitudes your students have regarding a particular medium. For example, if you show them an instructional television program, will they be inclined to think of the program as entertainment? If so, how will their perceptions affect their learning?

It is also important to consider your students' knowledge and skills in a particular area. What do your students already know about the content an instructional medium deals with? What content-related skills do your students already possess? In light of the answers to these questions, do you think that the instructional medium presents the content at a level that your students will be able to understand?

Also think about the general abilities of your students. If you are working with below-average learners, then it is likely that most of them will not be good readers. If that is the case, you should consider using nonprint media whenever appropriate. For example, if you were attempting to teach below-average learners how an automobile engine operates, the description of the process might best be presented by a medium that allows the learners to see and hear how the process works, rather than a medium that requires them to read about the process.

Instructional Activities

The question of whether a particular instructional medium should be used should also be examined in light of the instructional activity it is intended to present. Media differ with respect to their ability to present particular instructional activities. For example, when it comes to presenting information and providing examples, some media are capable of depicting motion and sound, and other media are not. So, if we are interested in describing, in words, how a steam engine operates, almost any medium can do the job. If, however, we are interested in accurately depicting how a steam engine works, our choice of media becomes much more limited; film or television might be the medium of choice, since both can accurately depict motion and present sounds.

In addition to differing in their ability to present information and provide examples, media often differ in the ways in which they can present other instructional activities. Let's look at each type of instructional activity and see how various media might be used to support it.

Motivating Students   As we indicated earlier, media are often used to help present this instructional activity. Many teachers have found that they can gain their students' attention by presenting them with interesting visual images ranging from simple black-and-white hand-drawn cartoons to lifelike images incorporating motion and color. A variety of media, such as motion pictures, filmstrips, television, computers, slides, charts, and transparencies can be used to present these images.

You may also gain your students' attention or arouse their curiosity by having them listen to various sounds, ranging from the sound of a famous person giving a speech to the sound of the wind during a hurricane. In order to present your learners with sounds such as these, a variety of media may be employed, including audio recording (on tapes, discs, or records), television, motion pictures, and slides syn-chronized with tapes.

Informing Students of Objectives   Teachers often will present their objec-tives to students orally and/or in writing via handouts, the chalkboard, or overhead transparencies. However, other media may also be employed for this purpose. For example, if most of the other instructional activities are to be delivered by a particular medium (for example, the computer), then it may be convenient to use that same medium to present your objectives.

Helping Students Recall Prerequisites   When you are reminding students of the prerequisites they need to recall, an oral statement will often suf-fice. However, a written reminder of the prerequisites may also be help-ful. Such a reminder might be presented via the chalkboard, an overhead transparency, or a written handout.

Presenting Information and Examples   The media you use in order to present information and examples to your students will depend, in large part, on the nature of the learning outcome you want your students to attain. Let's look at each type of outcome separately.

If your outcome falls in the knowledge domain, then it is important that you present that information to your students within a larger, more meaningful context. Media that can present visual images will often help. For example, rather than merely describing the physical characteristics of Abraham Lincoln to your students, it would be more effective to accom-pany such a description with pictures of the man. And, inasmuch as sounds may also broaden the context in which facts are presented, then media that present sounds to your learners may also help them to recall certain facts.

In the intellectual skills domain, a large number of outcomes require students to be able to identify different objects based upon their physical characteristics. This is one type of concept learning. An example would be having a student classify various plants based upon each plant's phys-ical features. In order to present students with the information and exam-ples necessary to make such classifications, visual media, such as slides or motion pictures, are often required.

Another type of outcome in the intellectual skills domain requires students to be able to describe the relationship among various things, events, or people (such as the familial relationship between an aunt and her niece). For outcomes of this sort, the use of charts, slides, or other media that can depict the relationship between abstract concepts is par-ticularly important.

Other major outcomes in the intellectual skills domain involve rule-using and problem-solving. Often the printed word is the best way of communicating the information and explaining the examples students need in order to be able to perform these sorts of skills. However, in some courses, students are using computer-accessed databases both to define and to solve problems.

In the motor skills domain, the instructional activity called "information and examples" often consists of a live explanation and demonstration. However, media such as motion pictures and television (videotape or videodisk) are particularly good media choices here in that both media possess motion, slow-motion, and stop-action capabilities. Other visual media, such as filmstrips and slides, can also be used for demonstrating motor skills, but their value is diminished somewhat by the fact that these media cannot depict motion.

Finally, in the attitude domain, it is quite valuable to have a person your students admire advocate a view or model a behavior you would like to see your students adopt. In many instances (particularly in the early grades), you the teacher will serve as the role model. On other occasions, respected individuals can be brought into the classroom, but more often than not, you will have to use other means in order to present such individuals to your students. For example, a videotape can be used to present a rock star speaking out against drug use.

In trying to convince students to adopt a particular point of view, messages presented via television or motion pictures may be most effective, inasmuch as these media are usually more capable than others in providing your students with a sense of reality, of being there. Certainly other media, such as audio recordings or slides with tapes, can effectively be used to present information or examples related to attitudes; however, since the former cannot present visual images and the latter cannot depict motion, they may not be as effective as television or motion pictures.

Now that we have discussed some media you might use when you are presenting information and examples to your students, let's turn to the next type of instructional activity.

Providing Practice and Feedback   The media you use to present your practice activities should be capable of providing the same conditions as described in your objective. For example, if your objective calls for your students to name various public officials when shown pictures of those officials, then the medium you use during your practice activity should be capable of presenting pictures.

Although some objectives may require that students respond to some pictures or sounds, many more objectives require that students respond to written questions. Therefore, many practice exercises will be presented via worksheets, chalkboards, or computers.

The computer is a particularly good medium for providing practice, especially for intellectual skills. The computer can easily provide an extensive variety of practice problems and, more important, adjust the amount, sequence, and difficulty of those problems in light of the student's performance.

Media differ with regard to their capability to provide feedback to students. Whereas some media can "judge" a student's response and provide response-specific feedback, other media usually only provide general feedback. This difference becomes particularly important when you are teaching intellectual skills or motor skills. When your students are practicing these skills, it is important that they receive response-specific feedback that not only indicates whether a response was correct or incorrect, but also provides information designed to help them correct any errors.

For intellectual skills outcomes, computers and interactive videodisks can serve as excellent sources of response-specific feedback. The latter medium can be particularly effective in depicting a real-life problem-solving situation (such as teaching a child how to deal with a bully), asking the viewer to choose from one of several ways to respond to the situation, and then presenting the probable consequences of responding in that fashion.

Most media (other than very expensive simulators) are not capable of providing learners with feedback that appraises the quality of the performance of a motor skill. With such skills, having an instructor observe and critique a student's motor-skill performance is the best means of providing response-specific feedback.

Summarizing the Lesson   In some cases, it is a good idea simply to present a lesson summary via the same medium that was used to present the bulk of a lesson. However, we believe that if you rely on other media to present most of a lesson, then it is often a good idea for you to interact with your students during the lesson summary. We make this recommendation because we know that in some cases, students view "mediated" lessons as being less important, as simply being an opportunity to relax. Getting the students to respond to some summary questions that you pose (these may be presented to the students before, during, or after the lesson) is an excellent way of ensuring that they will view the mediated lesson as a normal part of the instructional process, not simply a time-filler.

Choosing Media: An Example

We have discussed the three factors (practicality, student characteristics, and instructional activities) that you should consider before you decide to use a particular instructional medium. Now let's look at an example of how those factors might come into play.

Ms. Washington, the teacher we discussed in the problem scenario at the beginning of this chapter, is still wondering whether to use "Capital Ideas," the computer software program she read about. She thinks it might serve as a good means of providing her students with practice in learning the state capitals, but before she incorporates it into her instructional plan, she decides to consider it in terms of the three factors we have discussed in this chapter.

First, Ms. Washington examines whether it will be practical to use "Capital Ideas." Although her school does not own the program, the media center director informs Ms. Washington that the district media depository has several copies of the program and that it will be fairly easy to borrow those copies for a week. Another practical concern is that Ms. Washington's classroom is not equipped with any computers. However, the children in her class have access to the computers in the media center twice each week. Ms. Washington decides that during the week they are learning about state capitals, each child will have a sufficient opportunity to use the computer program. Thus, from a practical standpoint, "Capital Ideas" appears to be an appropriate instructional tool.

Second, Ms. Washington considers whether "Capital Ideas" is appropriate in light of the characteristics of the children in her class. The children have worked with instructional software before and seem to have enjoyed doing so. Furthermore, they seem to have learned the content the software programs were designed to help teach. However, Ms. Washington wonders whether this particular software program is appropriate in light of the skills, knowledge, and general ability level of her students. She decides she will preview the program before she makes any decision regarding this issue.

Third, Ms. Washington considers whether "Capital Ideas" is well suited to provide her students with practice in learning the state capitals. She knows that, in general, the computer can serve as a good means of providing students with practice, and the brochure she received about "Capital Ideas" indicates that the program is appropriate for that purpose. Nonetheless, she decides that when she previews the program, she will check to make sure it really will provide her students with the practice they need.

Having considered the three factors described above, Ms. Washington decides that she is likely to use "Capital Ideas" as part of her instructional plan for teaching her students the names of the state capitals. But she wisely decides to preview the program before she makes a final decision.

Computers in Instruction

Before we present you with some practice exercises, we would like to briefly discuss one instructional medium that is getting a great deal of attention—the computer. One of the reasons computers seem to be so popular may be because they are a relatively new educational tool. However, with rare exception, the novelty of computers should not be reason enough to employ them. Instead, we hope that before you decide to use the computer to present a particular instructional activity, you will consider the three factors (practicality, student characteristics, and instructional activities) we have been discussing in this chapter.

The question of practicality is important because in many schools, students have rather limited access to computers. In such situations, you must carefully consider scheduling so that students have access to the computer at the appropriate point in your instructional plan.

Is the computer likely to be an appropriate medium for your students in light of their characteristics? We have found that in most instances, students enjoy working with computers; they usually have little or no fear of the hardware. The crucial issue then becomes whether a particular software program is appropriate for your students in light of their skills, knowledge, and general ability.

The question of whether the computer is a good means of presenting a particular instructional activity can be examined both in terms of the capabilities of the computer itself (the hardware) and the characteristics of the instructional program (the software). With regard to hardware, the computer is a medium that can do a good job of presenting a variety of instructional activities. By being able to present games, colorful graphics, and a variety of encouraging messages to students, it can often be used as an excellent motivational device. In addition, it can be used to disclose print messages progressively, thus making it a good tool for providing learners with instructional information. Because the computer can pose questions and keep a record of student responses, it can serve as a testing device. It also can adjust the questions it poses to students, using the students' responses as the basis for that adjustment. Thus, it can be an excellent tool for presenting practice activities. And, as we have mentioned before, its ability to judge a student's response and provide the student with specific feedback further enhances its instructional value, especially when it comes to teaching intellectual skills. Yet, in spite of all it can do, the computer should not be viewed as the perfect medium; what it is capable of doing and what it is actually used for are usually two different things.

The instructional role a computer is playing at any particular time is determined by the type of instructional program (software) the computer is presenting at that moment. Many classification schemes have been used to categorize instructional software. One popular categorization scheme that is quite useful attempts to classify software into one of four categories, depending upon the primary instructional purpose of the software. These four categories are drill-and-practice programs, tutorial programs, simulations, and instructional games. Let's briefly discuss each of these categories.

Drill-and-practice programs are intended to provide students with the opportunity to practice skills or to rehearse the knowledge previously presented to them. Such programs are not intended to provide the initial information and examples students need to learn, and therefore should not serve as the only instruction. Instead, they should be used to reinforce a skill or information that has been presented to students through some other means.

In addition to providing students with practice, drill-and-practice programs usually present them with feedback regarding their performance. Effective drill-and-practice programs for objectives in the intellectual skills domain provide students with response-specific feedback. Moreover, such programs will take a student's previous responses into account when determining the sequence of questions that will be presented. Unfortunately, most drill-and-practice programs lack many of these features.

Whereas drill-and-practice programs focus on the instructional activity we call practice and feedback, *tutorial programs* focus on providing students with information and examples. Tutorial programs often are intended to serve as the primary means of instruction for a given objective, in that the programs provide students with information and examples that may enable them to acquire a particular skill or knowledge. Tutorials may also provide students with some opportunity to practice the behavior being taught, but the practice activities usually are not as extensive as those provided for by drill-and-practice programs. Although some tutorial programs have been designed or used by themselves for instruction, we have found that many tutorial programs must be used in conjunction with other instructional activities for students to acquire the skills or knowledge they are purported to teach.

Simulations are programs designed to provide learners with a simplified model of some aspect of the world. The simulation not only provides the learner with a model, it also gives the learner the opportunity to interact with that model in a lifelike manner. The results of using the model change as actions are taken by the learner. Thus, the learner has the opportunity to experience, in a safe environment, the likely real-world consequences of taking particular actions. For example, a simulation may present a student with a visual of an airplane cockpit and provide her with the opportunity to manipulate the aircraft's controls. As she does so, the program allows the student to experience (through pictures and sound) what would happen to the aircraft as a result of her actions.

Like drill-and-practice exercises, *instructional games* are programs that are designed to provide students with practice in performing a particular skill. Unlike regular drill-and-practice exercises, however, instructional games require the student to perform the skill within the context of a game. For example, one instructional game requires a student to shoot at incoming enemy aircraft, each of which has a simple addition problem written on its fuselage. In order to destroy the enemy aircraft, the student must solve the addition problems. When the student types in a correct answer, an enemy plane is destroyed; an incorrect response results in the destruction of one of the student's defending aircraft. In another game, as a child correctly matches shapes and colors, he or she is given the opportunity to create a colorful picture. These are but two examples of the many types of challenges presented by instructional games.

Although many students will enjoy playing the instructional games a computer can present, you should be alert to some possible shortcomings. First, some students may not be motivated by the challenge a game presents. Second, many games do not provide the detailed response-specific feedback necessary to teach intellectual skills. Third, on the poorest of computer games, it is not clear what skills are being taught. They appear only to be academic time-fillers, with no apparent educational value.

TABLE 5.1:

Objective: The student will correctly solve written word problems involving rate, time, and distance by using the formula $D = R \times T$

Type of Instructional Activity	Description
1. Motivation	a. show *videotape* reminding students of increase in state speed limits
	b. ask students: how can we figure out how long will it take to get to various places?
2. Objective	a. tell students they will solve word problems involving how far, fast, and long it takes to travel
3. Prerequisites	a. remind students that travel takes time
	b. remind students how to use an algebraic equation (e.g., $A = L \times W$)
4. Information and examples	a. explain concepts of rate, time, distance
	b. explain formula $D = R \times T$
	c. give examples of using each part of the formula as the unknown; use "real world" contexts (plane, train, etc.)
5. Practice and feedback	a. group students to work on set of 10 written problems
	b. review answers to problems with class
6. Additional examples	a. if needed, provide additional examples
7. Additional practice and feedback	a. if needed, give students additional problems to work on individually
	b. review answers to problems with class
8. Summary	a. Remind students: we have learned how to solve word problems involving rate, time, and distance.
	b. Ask students to state the formula for each type of problem covered.

PRACTICE

1. Table 5.1 is a copy of one of the lesson plans discussed in Chapter 4. As you can see, the teacher who developed the plan has decided that she will serve as the primary means of presenting

several of the instructional activities. Most of the other activities will be presented by a textbook, worksheets, or by some of the students in the class. However, in order to motivate her students, the teacher has decided to show them a videotape of a public service announcement designed to inform people of the new automobile speed limits. Identify some of the questions the teacher should have asked herself before she decided to use this medium.

2. Mrs. Brown usually has her students learn about the human circulatory system by having them read a chapter in their textbook. However, this year she is teaching a group of below-average learners and she thinks they will not understand the textbook description. She decides that instead of having them read the textbook, she will give them a lecture in which she describes how the circulatory system works. She also decides that she will create some simple overhead transparencies. Was her selection of an alternative instructional medium a good one? Provide a rationale for your answer. Be sure that your rationale deals with the issues of practicality, learner characteristics, and instructional activities.

3. Mr. Martinez is teaching the children in his kindergarten class to identify various shapes, and he feels they need more practice in this area. He decides that an appropriate solution to this problem will be to show the children an instructional film entitled *Ship-Shapes*. According to a promotional brochure, the film focuses on the adventures of a famous cartoon character who "sails through the Land of Shapes and discovers the characteristics of the shapes he encounters there." Has Mr. Martinez chosen an instructional medium that is well suited for providing the practice he thinks his students need? Provide a rationale for your answer.

4. Mrs. Oliver usually has her students learn about parallel and series electrical circuits by having them read a chapter in their textbook. However, she has just read a review that says that "Circuit Maker" is an excellent computer game that focuses on this topic. She decides she will have her students play this game rather than read the description in the textbook. Do you think "Circuit Maker" is appropriate for the instructional purpose Mrs. Oliver has in mind? Provide a rationale for your answers.

5. Mr. Hinson has just read a brief review of a software program called "Compass Finder." According to the review, "'Compass Finder' is a computer simulation that gives students the opportunity to learn how to use a compass to help them find their way across unmarked terrain, and they never even have to leave the classroom!" Mr. Hinson would like his students to become proficient at using a compass, but he is skeptical about using computers for instructional purposes. Most of the instructional soft-

ware he has seen could just as easily have been presented in print. Do you think that "Compass Finder" may be well suited for Mr. Hinson's instructional purposes? Provide a rationale for your answer.

FEEDBACK

1. Listed below are three general questions the teacher should have asked herself before she decided whether to use the videotape as part of her instructional plan. Listed beneath each general question are several more specific questions we think the teacher also should have asked. Don't be concerned by the number of questions we have listed; most of the questions related to choosing an instructional medium can be answered very quickly.

   A. Is the videotape practical to use in this situation?

      1. Is the videotape readily available?
      2. If the tape is not readily available, what will be the time and cost involved in obtaining it?
      3. Is a videotape player readily available?
      4. If a player is not readily available, what will be the time and cost involved in obtaining one?
      5. If there are expenses associated with showing the videotape, are there funds available to cover those expenses?
      6. Is there a convenient location in which the tape can be shown to my students?

   B. Is the videotape appropriate in light of my students' characteristics?

      1. What attitudes are my students likely to have about being shown this videotape?
      2. How will my students' attitudes affect their learning?
      3. Does the videotape discuss the new speed limits in a manner that my students are likely to understand?

   C. Is the videotape a good means of presenting the motivational activity for this lesson?

      1. Is the videotape likely to get my students thinking (gain their attention) about the new speed limits?
      2. Will the videotape plus my comments get the students interested in (arouse their curiosity about) figuring out how long it will now take to travel somewhere by car?

2. We agree with Mrs. Brown's decision to use overhead transparencies to help her describe how the human circulatory system

operates. Let's discuss her decision in terms of the three factors we have focused upon in this chapter.

From a practical point of view, the time and cost involved in producing simple transparencies should be minimal. The necessary hardware (an overhead projector) is likely to be readily available and can easily be employed in the classroom.

The overhead transparencies Mrs. Brown intends to employ seem to be appropriate in light of the characteristics of her students. Using pictures to supplement an oral description of the human circulatory system seems like a good instructional decision regardless of the type of learner involved; however, such a decision seems to be particularly appropriate when dealing with below-average learners, who are less likely to grasp a concept that is only presented orally.

It also appears that the overhead transparencies, serving as supplements to Mrs. Brown's oral presentation, are appropriate for the instructional activity she has in mind. Obviously, Mrs. Brown's lecture is intended to provide her students with information and examples related to the human circulatory system. She can use her overhead transparencies to help her elaborate upon (present a visual model of) the information she presents during her lecture.

3. The instructional film Mr. Martinez has chosen to use does not seem to provide his students with the practice he thinks they need. The film, as described in the quote from the promotional material, seems to present information about, and examples of, various shapes. However, there is no indication that the film will require the students to practice identifying shapes. Furthermore, when students are practicing an intellectual skill such as identifying shapes, it is important that they be given response-specific feedback. Even if practice opportunities were built into the film Mr. Martinez selected, the film would not be able to provide the students with such feedback.

4. Most instructional games are designed simply to provide students with practice in performing a particular skill; they are not usually intended to provide students with the information they will need in order to acquire that skill. Therefore, although the instructional game Mrs. Oliver has chosen may provide her students with excellent practice, it is unlikely that it will present them with the information they need to know about parallel and series circuits.

5. Simulations are programs designed to provide learners with a simplified model of some aspect of the real world and give the learners an opportunity to practice interacting with that model in a lifelike manner. Therefore, Mr. Hinson is likely to find that

the simulation program he has read about will present his learners with a chance to practice the skill he wants them to acquire without their having to leave the classroom. This practice opportunity cannot be provided by print materials. Mr. Hinson should seriously consider using the simulation as part of his instructional plan, which may, at a later point, also involve the students using a real compass.

APPLICATION

Choose the media you will use to present each of the instructional activities described in the two lesson plans you have been developing. Be sure to consider using some of the alternative media discussed in this chapter. Below each of the instructional activities in your lesson plans, list the media you will use to present that activity. Be prepared to provide a rationale for each medium you have chosen.

SUMMARY

In this chapter, we described how to decide whether to use a particular instructional medium as part of your instructional plan. Instructional media may be defined as the physical means by which instruction is delivered to students. The term *media hardware* refers to equipment, and the term *media software* refers to instructional materials presented via a piece of media hardware.

When you are choosing a means for presenting an instructional activity, in most cases you are likely to choose to present the activity yourself, via a textbook, or via supplementary print material such as a workbook. However, if you think you would like to use some other medium to present the activity, you should ask yourself whether the medium you are considering will be (a) practical to use, (b) appropriate for your students, and (c) a good means of presenting a particular instructional activity.

One instructional medium that is becoming increasingly popular is the computer. Computer software can be grouped into four categories, each intended to serve a different purpose: drill-and-practice programs, tutorial programs, simulations, and instructional games. By being aware of the purposes different categories of software typically serve, you will be better able to decide whether a particular piece of software is a good means of presenting a particular instructional activity.

Developing Assessment Tools

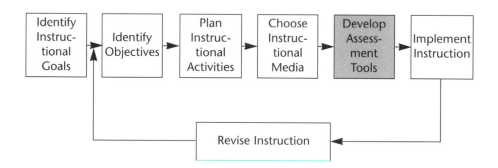

Tests and other assessment tools cannot be viewed separately from the instructional process. They are our means of assessing whether students have achieved our goals and objectives, and therefore, our tests must be consistent with our goals and objectives.

PROBLEM SCENARIO

Mr. Jefferson just completed a unit on the Russian Revolution and wants to test his students to find out how much they have learned. There is a test provided in the teacher's guide for the social studies textbook he is using. However, as he reviews the test, Mr. Jefferson notes that all of the test items are multiple choice and, for some reason, that bothers him. He can't decide whether to use the test or to write another one. How can he decide if the test items in the teachers' guide are appropriate? If they are not, what kind of items should he write?

CHAPTER OBJECTIVES

The objectives for this chapter are that you will be able to

1. describe the various purposes for using tests
2. determine if test items match objectives
3. describe the use of alternative assessment tools such as rating scales and portfolios
4. write assessments to match given objectives

BACKGROUND INFORMATION

The terms *testing* and *evaluation* are loaded with emotional connotation. We have encountered few people who really enjoy being tested or being evaluated. None of us, it seems, likes to be on the receiving end of tests. However, there is every indication that tests will continue to play an important role in education.

As more and more states become involved in identifying the competencies, or skills, that students in various grade levels must possess, the emphasis on a relatively new approach to testing has increased. This approach involves developing tests that are designed to determine whether students have acquired the various skills that have been identified in the competency statements. Although this manner of developing tests may seem quite reasonable, it is not the traditional way in which tests have been developed. The traditional approach involved creating very difficult items that could be used to rank students in terms of their knowledge of the content area. The items were never intended to be representative of all the knowledge and skills in the area.

Because the new approach to testing focuses on whether students have acquired specific skills, it is very important that the test items that are developed for such tests do assess a student's ability to perform the specified skills. In other words, a test item must measure a student's ability to perform the same behavior as specified in a particular objective. This is often called *objective-referenced* or *criterion-referenced* testing. Objective-referenced testing is also referred to as *authentic assessment* if it requires the student to perform the skill in the context in which the skill would be used outside the classroom. Classroom testing is usually only a proxy for what we really want students to be able to do. For example, if students were to master the skill of making a presentation, they would typically be asked to make a speech in class. However, an authentic assessment would require a student to make a speech before the local chamber of commerce or a church group in order to demonstrate mastery of this objective. The alternative assessment techniques that we discuss in this chapter (e.g., rating scales and portfolios) often can be used as tools for authentic assessment.

In this chapter, we will cover many familiar concepts in testing. We will focus on the development of test items and other assessment (testing) tools that *match* objectives by requiring students to demonstrate the behaviors described in given objectives. We will encourage you to consider alternative forms of assessment which require the student to use skills in relevant contexts.

We should also note our use of the terms *tests* and *assessments tools*. We typically think of tests as formal multiple-choice or essay exams that are given in most classes. However, *assessment tools* may be a better description of what we will be discussing in this chapter because *assessment tools* refers to a broad range of ways of determining if students can perform or have mastered an objective. We will use the terms *tests* and *assessment tools* interchangeably, referring in either case to means of determining student competence.

MAJOR CONCEPTS AND EXAMPLES

There are a number of reasons for testing students:

1. assigning grades to students
2. determining what students know in order to provide appropriate remediation
3. identifying ineffective portions of instruction

Perhaps the most common reason for testing is to assign grades. It is often assumed that the grading of students serves to motivate them to perform at their best. We are all aware of situations in which we have put in an extra effort in order to earn a particularly important grade. We cannot overlook the importance of grades as a motivating factor for many, but certainly not all, students.

Today, however, there are other important reasons for testing students. One is to determine student progress toward the achievement of particular skills. After taking a test designed for such purposes, students can be given specific feedback that is designed to help them master the skills they failed to attain. For example, on a test involving the addition of fractions with common denominators, it is noted that a student is adding the denominators as well as the numerators, incorrectly thinking that $1/4 + 1/4 = 2/8$. More important than a grade on this test is the specific feedback the student should receive. In the example with fractions, the nature of the student's error should be noted and he should be provided with a review of the proper way of adding two fractions with the same denominator. In this case, test items are not being used as a means of making a judgment about the student, but rather as a means of helping the student identify a weakness in his understanding of the content, and as a means of pointing the student in a direction that will be helpful in remediating that weakness.

In a similar fashion, test data can be used to help the teacher. Usually it can be assumed that when most of the students in a class do poorly on items for a particular objective, there has been something about the instruction that has gone wrong. Often the data from well-designed test items can help us pinpoint what those problems are and may suggest revisions that will make the instruction more effective in the future.

Testing can be used not only to motivate students and to assign them a grade, but can also be used very effectively to determine student progress in achieving certain skills and to provide appropriate remediation. Furthermore, tests can be used to provide data to teachers to improve their instruction.

Who Develops Tests?

Professionals who work for companies that produce tests or for state-level testing programs spend much of their time writing and revising test items. They have to create large pools of test items and to examine the data from thousands of students who have taken the tests. In addition to the items prepared by these professional test-makers, many test items are written by textbook writers who provide test items for the chapters in their books. These test items usually appear in the teachers guide for the text. It is important to note, however, that textbook writers are not necessarily expert test writers and the items that they produce may or may not be good assessments of the behaviors they are trying to teach. Furthermore, in many textbook series, the test items that appear in the accompanying teachers guides may be written not by the textbook authors but by others who may not be totally familiar with the content of the text.

Another source of test items is the classroom teacher. Teacher education programs have traditionally included little, if any, formal training in the development of test items. Most teachers, because of this lack of training, have inadequate understanding of the concepts underlying sound test development and, consequently, end up developing tests like those that their teachers gave them. We hope that the new approach to developing test items, as described in this chapter, will begin to remedy this situation and that you will see the critical interrelationship between testing and instruction.

Matching Test Items to Objectives

A good test item is one that measures what it is intended to measure. This is basically the concept of the *validity* of a test or a test item. Putting this thought into terms we have been working with, if there is a match between the behavior described in an objective and the behavior assessed by a test item designed to measure student attainment of that objective, then it may be said that the test item is valid. For example, if an objective indicates that "the student will be able to add two two-digit numbers," then a valid test item would be one that requires the student to add two two-digit numbers. It would be inappropriate to ask students to add two three-digit numbers. Is the validity of the item affected by whether the two numbers are listed vertically or horizontally? Not unless the objective specifies the way in which the numbers should be arranged.

In a system of the sort presented in this book, you begin with goals and objectives, and your objectives then serve as the basis upon which to develop test items. The verb in an objective describes the kind of behavior that you expect from your learners and that you would assess on a test. For example, if the objective states that the student will be able to "list," then we would expect that the test item in turn would ask the student to "list" some information. While it is not always possible to use the verb in the objective directly in the construction of the test items, it does give us the key as to which kind of item will be appropriate to measure the objective.

It is also important that the conditions you include in your test items match the conditions specified in your objectives. Earlier, we used the example of giving a speech. The conditions under which this is done could vary greatly and might influence the ability of the student to perform. Clearly, giving the speech at home would probably be much easier than giving it to a group that the student has never met. However, in fact, speeches are often given to groups in which we know only a few people. Therefore, your objective should indicate that the speech will be delivered under those conditions, and you should make sure that you assess students under those conditions.

Assessment Tools for the Various Types of Learning Outcomes

Let's review the four domains of objectives and the kinds of items that are most often used to assess the objectives in those domains.

Assessment Tools for Knowledge Objectives

Knowledge objectives require students to recognize or recall information that they have already encountered. Here we are asking the student to either state, describe, or list some information or to select from an array of possible answers, such as would be the case with a multiple-choice question. Therefore, knowledge items might require the student to list the two primary political parties in the United States or to select, from a list, the food with the highest amount of carbohydrates. In the first case we are requiring the student to generate the answer by completing a question, and in the second case we are asking the student simply to recognize the information. In both cases, we are assuming that the specific information has been taught and it is a matter of recalling or recognizing it.

Assessment Tools for Intellectual Skills Objectives

Here again, we find ourselves predominately using either multiple-choice or completion test items. Typically, when the objective has to do with learning about concepts, we can use multiple-choice items in which the student is required to select examples of that concept. For example, if we were to have an objective stating that children will be able to recognize those animals that are members of the cat family, we could provide a question in which the names or pictures of various animals are presented and we could ask the student to select, or identify, those in the cat family.

As we move to the next level of intellectual skills, namely rule using, we are more likely to have the students complete an answer rather than to pick a multiple-choice answer, although that is not always the case. For example, suppose we want our students to use rules to determine how to set a boat's sail in order to reach a certain point when they are given the current position of the boat and the direction of the wind. Our first choice would be to ask each student to sail a boat actually under various conditions. This action would combine a motor skill with an intellectual skill. If this is not possible, then we would have to consider less direct indications of their skills. We would either assess our students' ability to perform this task by listing a number of sail positions and asking the students to select the correct one or to describe the correct sail position. In either case, we would be asking the students to use a rule in order to determine how to set the sail.

If we progress to the next level of intellectual skills, namely problem solving, then we are even more likely to have students respond to a completion item. For example, we may want our students to be able to describe how to navigate a sailboat around a land mass in order to reach a point on the other side. In all likelihood, we would write an item in which they would be given a description of a situation with a sailboat, and they would be asked to describe how they would sail it.

What about a problem-solving task such as creating a science project or writing an essay? The use of a checklist or rating scale to evaluate these products would be appropriate.

Assessment Tools for Motor Skills Objectives

In many situations, a relatively informal approach is taken to assessing motor skills. The instructor simply observes students performing the skill and decides whether they have or have not been successful. Whether or not the instructor is aware of it, he or she is, in fact, using a mental checklist to determine if the student has been successful. A more objective approach would be to have a written set of criteria, in the form of a checklist or rating scale, available for judging the adequacy of each student's performance. The checklist or rating scale might simply be a list of the characteristics of what you would consider to be a successful performance. For example, a checklist for assessing the adequacy of a tennis serve might include such items as "Was the ball tossed upwards properly?" "Did the learner fully extend his or her arm during the swing?" "Did the ball clear the net?" and "Did the ball land in the appropriate section of the court?"

When developing such checklists, you should be certain to list each of the major steps necessary to perform the motor skill. It is not easy to determine exactly what is meant by a major step, and we can obviously err in the direction of having too few or too many steps in our checklist. Nonetheless, when you develop a checklist to assess the performance of a motor skill, the important thing is to try to identify those critical components that are likely to result in either success or failure in the overall performance of the skill.

With any motor skill, the objective should indicate whether we are evaluating the process itself (that is, the execution of the skill), the result of the performance of the skill, or both (as was the case in our tennis serving example). For example, if we are teaching diving, it is almost certain that the performance of the various components of the dive will be evaluated in order to determine whether the student has been successful or not. On the other hand, if we are judging a student's ability to make a ceramic pot, we might not be as concerned with the specific steps that are followed in the process of making the pot, but rather would make our assessment on the basis of the quality of the final product, the pot. These are decisions which you, the teacher, must make as you develop your objectives and the assessments for them.

Assessment Tools for Attitude Objectives

As we have indicated earlier, we consider attitudes to be feelings and beliefs that are reflected in tendencies to act in particular ways in given situations. First of all, it is critical that students actually have the behaviors that we wish them to demonstrate. Then we can determine if they choose, in fact, to execute those behaviors. Therefore, when assessing an attitude it is important to provide the student with a situation in which that attitude or the behavior that reflects that attitude would be appropriately displayed. Usually, this can best be assessed through direct observation.

We may also wish to assess our students' knowledge of the situation as it is related to their attitudes. For example, if we attempted to teach attitudes about religious freedom and religious tolerance, we might want to provide some test items dealing with our students' knowledge of the various religious faiths that they might encounter in their city. This would indicate if they are even aware of the religious beliefs of which we would like them to be tolerant. If we wanted to teach young children to share, we would want to determine if they could describe what it means "to share." However, it is extremely important to note that assessing knowledge about an attitude *is not assessing the attitude.* The only real assessment is demonstration of a preference on the part of the student for the behaviors that are representative of the attitude. Being able to describe the various religions that might be found in a town or city is *not equivalent* to respecting religious practices among people with religious beliefs that differ from those of the student. In this situation, *what* is assessed, and *where,* or under what conditions, make all the difference in the world between demonstrating mastery of an abstract set of concepts and demonstrating real understanding.

Our purpose for reviewing the various domains of learning outcomes with regard to testing is to point out that the first step in developing the test items for any objective is to identify what domain the objective is in. Once you have done so, you can narrow down the type of item that would best assess the behavior described in the objective. We have summarized this information below.

Typical Testing Procedures

Domain	Types of Assessment Tools
Knowledge	Multiple choice, completion
Intellectual Skills	Multiple Choice, completion; essay or product (with checklist or rating scale)
Motor Skills	Checklist or rating scale
Attitudes	Observation of behavior, questionnaire about behavior

We can use this summary to help us consider the problem posed in the opening scenario in which Mr. Jefferson is bothered that the items provided in his teachers guide are all multiple choice. We know that he should examine the relationship between his specific objectives and the items and determine if there is a match. There may well be a match, and items should not be criticized simply because they are in a multiple-choice format. If, however, Mr. Jefferson finds that the objectives and items don't match, then he will have to write new ones. The techniques for doing so are discussed in the next section.

Guidelines for Developing Assessment Tools

In this brief text we cannot provide a complete set of rules on how to develop various types of tests and test items. We encourage you to check other sources to get a more thorough understanding of this process.

Nonetheless, it is our contention that the most crucial step in test-item construction is being aware of the behavior described in an objective and writing test items that assess a student's ability to perform that behavior. In writing such items, however, it is important to know some of the basic rules, or guidelines, of good test-item construction. Therefore, in the paragraphs that follow we will provide you with some basic information that should help you to develop very appropriate test items for classroom testing purposes. First we will discuss guidelines for pencil-and-paper types of assessment tools. Then we will discuss guidelines for alternative assessment tools, such as using rating scales for observations.

Pencil-and-Paper Assessment Tools

If the behavior in your objective indicates that the student will "identify" or "select" something, then often a multiple-choice item or series of multiple-choice items can be used to assess the student. When developing multiple-choice items there are two very basic rules to follow. The first rule is to put as much information as possible in the stem, that is, that portion of the question that the students read before they select their answer. In other words, don't put just a few words in the stem and then load up all of the alternatives with many words. In fact, do just the reverse. Try to minimize the length of the alternatives.

Good item:

In the United States, airplane speed is most enhanced by the wind when planes are flying in which direction?

1. north
2. south
3. east
4. west

Poor item:

Planes fly

1. slower when they head north
2. faster when they head west
3. faster when they fly east
4. about the same speed regardless of direction

The second rule in developing multiple-choice items is to have all of the alternative answers approximately the same length, with none of them containing particular cues that will result in someone choosing the correct answer without really knowing it.

Good item:

In the story *Mrs. Smith Went to Arizona,* her primary concern seemed to be

1. her financial security
2. her sons and daughters
3. her job prospects
4. her home and neighborhood

Poor item:

If John rode his bike for 2½ hours at a steady rate of 15 miles per hour, to the nearest ½ mile, how far would he go?

1. 30 minutes
2. 35 blocks
3. 37.5 miles
4. 40 hours

(Can you figure out why this is a poor item?)

If the behavior in your objective indicates that the student will "name" or "state" something, then a completion item is appropriate. When developing completion items, it has been our experience that you can get a much better indication of what students really know by asking them to respond to specific questions rather than completing a statement by filling in a blank space. For example, rather than asking students to complete the statement "The Battle of the Bulge was fought in ———," it would be better to ask the students: "In what year was the Battle of the Bulge fought?" The completion question could be answered with either a date or a location.

If your objective calls for the student to "discuss," "describe," or "explain" something, then an essay question is the type of test item you should employ. Frequently, the item can be worded using much the same language as the objective. For example, if the objective states that "The student will describe the ecological principles that should be employed to maintain a marsh area," then your essay question might simply state, "In two or three paragraphs, describe the ecological principles that should be employed to maintain a marsh area." An essay question does not necessarily require a long, complicated answer.

In addition to developing the essay question itself, you should also develop a list of criteria you will use to determine whether or not the student has correctly answered the question. For example, before your students respond to the essay question about marshes, you should have a clear idea of the features of the answer you want them to list. Perhaps one such feature would be that the student clearly described three of the ecological principles discussed in class.

With attitude objectives, if we can't actually observe the student making an attitudinal choice, we will use a questionnaire. Such questionnaires consist of items that do not necessarily have a right or wrong answer but rather measure how students feel about various topics or activities. Much has been written about questionnaire construction. The most important aspect is to avoid writing questions that will lead students to respond as they think you want them to (by giving you the socially acceptable answer), rather than in accordance with how they really feel. In other words, the questionnaire should be as value-free as possible and should provide the respondents with the opportunity to describe honestly what they do or how they feel. If a student is filling out a questionnaire in which there is a clear indication of what the socially acceptable or desired answer is, the tendency is to give that answer or to give no answer at all.

A good item to ask on a questionnaire related to a human relations objective:

> Give an example of a situation that occurred this week in which you helped another student with a problem.

Poor items to ask on a questionnaire related to a human relations objective:

> Were you cheerful when working with other students this week?
> Do you believe that everyone should be treated the same?

(Why do you think these are poor questionnaire items?)

Alternative Assessment Tools

We have presented guidelines for the development of pencil-and-paper assessment tools. Now we need to turn to alternative assessment formats that you may be called upon to use, namely observations and ratings.

Perhaps the most unobtrusive and easiest-to-perform assessment is direct observation of students. The issue becomes: what is being observed? Observation usually takes place after direct instruction has occurred, and students are practicing what they have learned. This practice can vary from verbal information practice sheets, to such intellectual skills as mapmaking, to motor skills in a physical education class, to preferred behaviors reflected in an attitude objective. The major purpose of teacher observations is to provide feedback to the learner on the adequacy of the performance and to provide remediation as required. If too many students are experiencing the same problem, the teacher may want to resume direct instruction on the skills in question.

We haven't really answered our question on what is being observed. It should be the behavior described in the objective. Sometimes such observation is very easy, as in verbal information questions or intellectual skills problems, but what about the preparation of a project or writing an essay? Teachers usually use a *holistic assessment* approach, meaning that they get an overall impression of each student's progress and then make comments that seem appropriate. There are some problems with this relatively unstructured approach.

In essence, when observing any student behavior, the teacher should have either a written or internalized checklist of items to be reviewed. What characteristics of the essay that the student is writing are reflected in the objective? Is the emphasis on writing style or on the content? Should the teacher be looking for errors in fact or inference or in paragraph formation? These may seem to be obvious considerations, but it is easy to lose sight of what is important in the observation process if the behaviors to be observed are not made explicit.

Since observation is such a common form of informal evaluation, we should add another reason for indicating what is being observed, namely the possibility of bias. Most teachers would immediately insist that they are not biased, but research suggests that they do respond differently to different students. Where this is sometimes most obvious is with high- and low-ability students. High-ability students can get a halo effect, while the low students always do something wrong—or so it seems. Observation, when you know the students so well, lends itself to this kind of bias, namely, giving feedback based on who the student is rather than what the student has done. Having a list of behaviors or characteristics will help to eliminate this often unintentional form of bias.

What should the teacher do if the goal of a unit is for the student to develop an original product of some sort—either intellectual or physical—or the emphasis is on performing a skill that is represented in a series of steps to be completed, such as a dance? When an objective requires the student to demonstrate a process or to produce a product, it is almost always appropriate to assess the process or product with a rating scale.

A *rating scale* consists of two essential components: a list of the steps in the process or the characteristics of the product, and a scale for rating each step or characteristic. You can get an idea of what one is like by thinking about the questions that might have been asked on a form in a restaurant or hotel room. Often the guest is asked to rate each of a number of aspects of the service as excellent, good, ok, poor, or unacceptable. This is a good example of a rating scale for evaluating either a service or a product. A teacher can use the same kind of form to evaluate students' performance on a variety of instructional objectives.

Let's look at an example in which we must evaluate student project reports. These are written in many different courses. If your objective indicated that the student would be able to write a project report, how would you evaluate it? First, you would refer to the objective to determine if any criteria were stated there. Were content, length, style, and/or use of references listed among the criteria? If so, your rating scale would include these items. Did you indicate in the instruction that the report should have several major parts: introduction, description of resources used, indication of major points, and persuasive closing? If so, these items should also be on your rating scale.

Continuing our example, we may want to evaluate each of the major components of the report as well as appropriate content, length, style, and references. We probably want to make *two* decisions about each of these components: Is it present? How good is it? Therefore, for each item on our scale we want to indicate presences and quality, and we do so by creating a scale for rating the items. See Figure 6–1 for an example of how a rating scale might look for evaluating a project report using the identified criteria. Obviously, you could list any criteria that are important to you with regard to either a process or a product. Remember to communicate these criteria to the students so that they are aware of how they will be assessed.

Imagine that you have a set of reports to be graded. You would fill out one rating scale for each student. It is possible to add up the scale points in order to get a total score, and the range of scores can be used to assign grades. Or you can determine in advance that if a student obtains a certain number of points, he or she will be given a certain grade.

Another use of the completed rating forms is to determine what steps in the process or characteristics of the materials produced by the students were done most poorly. Where did the students seem to have problems

FIGURE 6-1
Evaluation of Project Report

Student Name _____ Date _____

	Inadequate or Missing 0	Adequate 1	Good 2	Excellent 3
Content				
Style				
Length				
Reference List				
Introduction				
Description of Resources				
Major Points				
Persuasive Closing				
Total				

and thereby lose points? This aspect will be important information that we will discuss in more detail in Chapter 8.

Another alternative assessment tool is a portfolio of the products that a student develops in a course. Many teachers are now using portfolios as a major component of the evaluation process and as a vehicle for communicating both with students and parents about the progress that the student is making in the course.

A *portfolio* is a collection of the work of a particular individual. Many professionals have portfolios that they use to show clients the kinds of work that they do. The portfolio serves the same purpose for the student and the teacher—it includes examples of the kind of work that is being done by the student in the class.

In most courses, each student will have a file folder that contains samples of the student's work. The samples could be traditional tests or reports, computer printouts, photographs, or other products that reflect the objectives of the course. You can decide in advance what items will go in the portfolio for all students, or you can negotiate individually with the students to identify their very best work for inclusion in the folder.

If individual students are pursuing individual goals and objectives in your course, these differences can be easily reflected in the portfolios. Portfolios should include work that indicates what the students knew or could do when they started the class and how their skills have developed over time. The greatest value of the portfolio is that it reflects the *changes* in the students as the skills grow more numerous and sophisticated. Comparisons of items in the portfolio should be chosen to reflect these changes.

Typically each item in the portfolio is evaluated as it is produced by the student. A second and more broad evaluation can take place as the portfolio is viewed over longer periods of time such as a six-week grading period or a semester. It can provide the basis for constructive discussions between you and the student and the student's parents about the strengths of the student's performance in the course. While constructive criticism can be provided to the student on the basis of the products in the portfolio, the major focus for the student should be the accomplishments reflected by the portfolio. As with any other assessment tool, the teacher can learn from the things that the majority of the students *did not learn,* as reflected in their portfolios. This information can be used to strengthen the instruction with the next group of students.

How Is a Test Developed?

In our discussion thus far, we have been primarily focusing on individual test items or scales and the importance of reflecting the behavior described in an objective. However, at some point, items must be put together in the form of a test. In this regard, there are two extremely important decisions that must be made by you, the test developer. The first includes the length and specificity of the directions that accompany the test, and the second involves determining how many items are to be included.

We are all frustrated at times by vague instructions at the beginning of a test. We are already a little anxious about having to take the test and perhaps somewhat insecure about our knowledge about what is being tested. Now we read the directions and find out that we really don't know what we are being asked to do.

We can't overemphasize the importance of being extremely explicit, clear, and simple with the directions for any test that you are going to develop. For example, you should let students know such things as whether they should attempt to answer every question, how much time they will have to complete the test, and the point value of each test item or cluster of test items. This is the kind of information you would want if you were taking a test, and your students certainly should have it as well.

An equally important question is how many test items are needed to determine if your students have really mastered your objectives. While there is no hard and fast answer to this question, there are some rules of thumb that have evolved over time by people who have developed classroom tests, and these rules are related to the four domains of learning. In the knowledge domain, if our objective is to identify the capital of the state of Texas, then there is basically only one question we can ask a student about this objective, namely, "What is the capital of the state of Texas?" We might use a completion item or we might use multiple choice, depending on how the objective is stated, but we certainly would not ask that question more than once. In general, then, if your objective involves the recall or recognition of knowledge, then you need ask only one question for each fact you hope your students have memorized. If the number of facts is quite large, then you will have to test only a sample of those facts.

If your objective involves an intellectual skill, then it is likely that more than one item will be needed to determine if your students have mastered the objective. To be more specific, it has often been suggested that at least three items be used to assess student attainment of an intellectual skill. If we refer to our objective of adding two two-digit numbers, we might use three items like these:

$$1. \quad \begin{array}{r} 43 \\ +52 \end{array} \qquad 2. \quad \begin{array}{r} 37 \\ +55 \end{array} \qquad 3. \quad \begin{array}{r} 51 \\ +89 \end{array}$$

If a student can respond correctly to two of these three items, then the student probably is not guessing but has actually mastered the intellectual skill. While the role of chance may be operating, particularly in multiple-choice situations, there is sufficient evidence to suggest that three items is sufficient for typical classroom testing of an intellectual skill.

Now let's consider a motor skill. While you have developed a checklist that describes the steps in executing that procedure and/or describes the quality of the product that will result from that motor skill, you still must determine how many times the student will be asked to perform the behavior. You may have decided this when you wrote the criterion portion of your objective, but regardless of whether you did so or not, the key question you must ask yourself is "How many times (or what percentage of the time) must a student perform this behavior correctly before I am satisfied that the student really mastered the skill?" Unfortunately, there are no rules for answering this question, so you must rely on your own judgment and experience.

As indicated earlier, an attitude is usually assessed either through observation or through the use of an attitude questionnaire. If we observe the student, we must decide how many times he or she must choose a particular behavior before we are willing to say that the student has acquired the desired attitude. If we use an attitude questionnaire, our decision is even harder. We must decide how we will tabulate the student's responses and how we will interpret the results of that tabulation. Again, there are no specific rules to follow in this situation. As you can see, accurate assessment of student attitudes is a particularly difficult issue.

While we have posed our problem as one of "How many items do we need to put on a test?" the real question we are asking is "What does the student have to do to convince me that he or she has mastered the skill described in the objective?" It is the answer to *this* question that then determines the number of items or repetitions of a behavior that you will require. This approach of "What will it take to demonstrate mastery?" should be the first question you ask when developing a test.

One of the important factors in determining the success of a test is trying out that test in advance with one of your learners or someone who is similar to those learners. It has been our experience that there are often as many or more problems with the tests given in an instructional setting as there are with the instruction itself. Since we are going to make important decisions about our learners and the quality of our instruction on the basis of our test data, it is critically important that the test items say what we want them to say. The best way of determining whether this is so is to try out test items with learners.

When you are constructing a test and you know what the right answer is, it is easy to believe that a test item says exactly what you think it says. However, when your words are translated onto paper and are typed and appear before the student, it is absolutely amazing how many alternative interpretations can be given to something that you think is very straightforward. Therefore, it is exceedingly important that any test that you develop be tried out with someone, preferably a student like those in your class. Perhaps you can use a student who was in your class the previous year. In addition, trying your test with another teacher or a secretary will often prove to be helpful. In short, have someone else help find the inevitable problems that appear in any instrument of this sort. Use that person's reactions to revise and improve your test in order to make sure it really is testing that which you think it is testing.

PRACTICE

1. Describe at least three major purposes for testing students after they have completed instruction.
2. Listed below are a number of objectives (with the criteria omitted) and test items. In each case, indicate if the test item adequately measures the objective. If not, write a better test item.

A. *Objective:* Define justice.
   Test item: Define justice.
B. *Objective:* Describe the two-party system.
   Test item: Select the party of the current president of the United States:

   a. Democrat
   b. Republican
   c. Labor
   d. Independent

C. *Objective:* From a given list of food items, identify foods that are high in sugar.
   Test item: Circle the foods listed below that are high in sugar:

   a. bananas
   b. potatoes
   c. chocolate
   d. orange juice

D. *Objective:* Be able to convert from scientific to standard notation.
   Test item: State the rule for converting from scientific to standard notation.
E. *Objective:* Given a hypothetical monthly income, the student will be able to allocate funds realistically to basic items in the family budget.
   Test item: In the United States, how much money is required per month to live at a minimum standard of living?
F. *Objective:* Students will appreciate classical music.
   Test Item: List the names of at least three famous classical composers and the title of at least one of their compositions.

3. Listed below are six objectives. Read each objective carefully and then write a test item that you think would assess that objective.

A. Given a map of the state of Florida, locate the major cities.
B. Be able to execute a successful serve in volleyball.
C. Be able to state the second law of thermodynamics.
D. Be able to discuss the impact of high technology on the economy of the state of California.
E. Be able to develop a plan for implementing instruction for a particular objective.
F. Choose to be an effective team member.

FEEDBACK

1. One of the major purposes of testing is to evaluate students in order to assign them grades or to determine an award-winner, but other purposes related to instruction may be of equal importance. One such purpose is to provide feedback to learners, particularly about skills they have not performed well. This feedback can help students identify the remediation they need in order to improve their performance. Another purpose of testing is to provide feedback to the teacher about ineffective instruction that should be improved before the next time it is presented.

2. The items relating to the definition of justice (objective A) and the identification of food that is high in sugar (objective C) seem to be appropriate.

   Objective B called for students to describe the two-party system. The test item, however, merely asked the students to identify the political party of the president. Obviously, the behavior called for by the test item does not match the behavior specified in the objective. An appropriate test item for this objective would have been an essay question asking students to describe the two-party system.

   Because objective D indicated that the student would actually compute the answer by converting from scientific notation to standard notation, it was inappropriate to ask the student to simply state the rule for doing so. We often mistakenly believe that if a student can state a rule, then the student should be able to apply it. However, research has indicated that this is simply not the case. Sometimes students can state the rule but not actually apply it, and in other cases, we find that students can apply rules, but they become confused when asked to state them. Therefore, in this particular case, the appropriate test item would have been a number expressed in scientific notation and directions asking the student to convert that number to standard notation.

   The test item for objective E asked students to indicate how much money is required to have a minimum standard of living. This does not assess a student's ability to allocate funds realistically to basic items in a family budget, which was the behavior specified in our objective. It would have been much more appropriate to give the student a monthly dollar figure and a list of standard household budgetary items, such as housing, transportation, clothing, and food, and ask the student to distribute the dollars across those categories.

The test item for F is not an effective way to determine if students have achieved what, in effect, is an attitude objective. Students must be able to recognize who the classical composers are, but knowing this information doesn't mean that they "appreciate" it. What would indicate their appreciation? Perhaps you wrote that you would observe if they chose to go to concerts or checked audiotapes out of the library. Behavior of this type would be a better indicator of their achievement of this objective than would listing information.

In those cases in which the test items we provided were inappropriate, you may have written new ones that were somewhat different from the ones we suggested here. The item you wrote may very well be appropriate, provided that it called for the same behavior as specified in the given objective.

3. It is impossible to list *the* correct test item for each of the objectives provided. However, we can suggest the kind of items we think would be appropriate and you can check your answers against ours.

   A. A good item would include a road map of the state of Florida, with all of the cities shown in their proper location. The directions for the item would ask the student to circle the major cities in the state. Perhaps the directions would also indicate the number of major cities that were to be circled. Another possibility, requiring a more difficult behavior on the part of your students, would be to give them a blank outline map of the state of Florida and ask them to list the name of each major city and place an X next to the location of each one. Clearly there is room for interpretation as to what the word *locate* means in this particular situation.

   B. We would hope that you would develop a checklist that would indicate the major steps in executing an effective serve in volleyball. Your checklist would probably involve such things as holding the ball, throwing the ball in the air, moving the arm in a particular pattern with the eventual result of having the ball arrive in the desired area on the other side of the net. This is an example of a motor skill in which both the process and the result, or outcome, can be judged. You must decide if both the process and the result must be acceptable.

C. In stating the second law of thermodynamics, it would be quite appropriate simply to ask the student to "state the second law of thermodynamics," and leave a blank space for the answer.

D. The objective indicates that students will be able to discuss the impact of high technology on California's economy. We assume that this is a knowledge objective that is simply asking students to recall information that they have learned from the text or from classroom discussions. Therefore the test item can be written in a fashion almost identical to that of the objective, namely, "Discuss at least four important ways in which the introduction of high technology has affected the economy of the state of California." Then leave space for the student to respond to this question.

E. In asking the student to develop a plan for implementing instruction for a particular objective, you would state the question in a fashion very similar to the objective. However, you would have to decide who chooses the content of the objective, you or the student. In other words, you might state that the student should develop an instructional plan for teaching long division, or you might state that the student should develop an instructional plan for any objective he or she chooses. In any event, you would want to have, for your own purposes, a rating scale that would (a) list the components that students should include in their instructional plan and (b) describe the criteria you would use to judge the adequacy of the components. You could then use this rating scale to judge each student's plan.

F. You could use a number of different approaches to assessing whether a student was choosing to be a good team member, but we would recommend an observational rating scale. The scale would include such items that describe how the student would respond in the team settings as: assists others with their tasks, and provides constructive comments. These behaviors should be stated in the positive and could be rated in terms of rarely to frequently observed. What would not seem to be appropriate for this objective is having a test on "teaming" or asking a group to turn in a project on the topic. However, assuming that you had provided students with instruction on how to participate effectively on teams, it would be possible to assess the objective at the same time that students were working in teams on an intellectual or motor skills objective.

APPLICATION

At this point, you have developed two lesson plans, each related to one objective. Now write a sufficient number of assessment items for each of your objectives. For some objectives, you may need to develop several items, while for others, one item will certainly be enough. Put the items together in one assessment instrument, and provide directions to the student at the top of the instrument.

Some of your objectives may emphasize procedures or the creation of products. If this is the case, create a checklist or rating scale that reflects the steps in the procedure or the characteristics of the product. Also indicate the various ratings that would be applied to the behaviors.

After you have completed the instrument, have a student who might receive your instruction, or someone else, review your test items. See if the person can explain what he or she thinks is being asked in each of your items. Make appropriate revisions in your test items based on the observations of this person.

SUMMARY

In this chapter we have reviewed the overall importance of testing in the process of designing instruction. We have emphasized the fact that test items are extremely important for providing students with an assessment of their progress in mastering objectives and that test results provide teachers with information regarding the quality of the instruction they have presented, as well as suggest how instruction might be revised in the future.

When we are using a systematic approach to planning instruction, the most important characteristics of a test item are that it matches the behavior described in the objective the test item is intended to test and that it reflects the conditions in which students will use these skills later on. We have provided various rules of thumb for developing pencil-and-paper, as well as alternative, assessment items and for combining them into tests. We also discussed the value of creating portfolios of student products that reflect the progressive development of their skills.

CHAPTER 7

Implementing Instruction

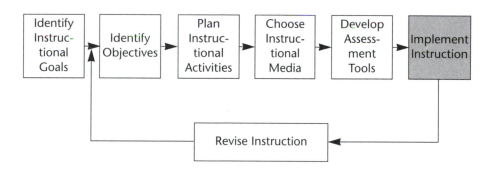

At this point, you have developed two lesson plans to help students acquire two learning outcomes, and you have developed assessment items to ascertain whether they have attained those outcomes. Now it is time for you to try out, or implement, the lesson plans and assessment items you have developed. How will you do so?

Assume for a moment that your lesson plans and assessment items will be part of a larger instructional unit. If you employ a traditional approach to instruction, these lessons will be two of many that are included in the unit. When the unit is over, it is likely that you will use your assessment items as part of a larger test designed to determine how much your students learned during the unit. Then, after you administer the test, you are likely to move on to the next unit. This sequence of instructional activities and testing activities is used in most classrooms and is likely to be representative of the sequence you will employ when you become a teacher. In this chapter, however, we will describe an alternate approach to implementing your instructional activities and your tests.

PROBLEM SCENARIO

Mr. Vallano has just administered the midterm examination in his college-prep math course and is very surprised and disappointed in the fact that his students have done so poorly. Although this is the first time he has formally assessed his students this semester, prior to the exam he was confident that most of them were learning the skills he wanted them to acquire. Indeed, whenever he had asked them questions in class, at least a few of his students were able to come up with the right answers. Moreover, most of the homework assignments the students had handed in contained very few errors. Yet, many of the students performed very poorly on the exam; in fact, quite a few of them were unable to answer the questions covering the basic skills Mr. Vallano had taught at the beginning of the semester. Now Mr. Vallano wonders what went wrong. Could he have implemented his instruction in a manner that would have enabled him to spot and correct these problems sooner?

CHAPTER OBJECTIVE

The objective of this chapter is that you will be able to describe how you might employ a mastery learning approach in a given learning situation.

BACKGROUND INFORMATION

The "traditional" sequence of instructional activities and assessment activities described in the introduction to this chapter has been labeled *group instruction* and is shown in Figure 7.1. As depicted, the teacher presents a unit of instruction to the entire class (or group) and then assesses the group and moves on to the next unit, where the cycle is repeated. As we stated earlier, this sequence of activities is very common and is likely to be the sequence you will employ in your classroom. However, it is important to note that under group instruction, all the students in a class participate in the same instructional activities at the same time. Since some students are able to learn more rapidly than others, the group-instruction approach usually results in a wide range of student performance on tests. A few of the students do very well, a few do very poorly, and most of them end up somewhere in the middle.

In recent years, various attempts have been made to tailor instruction to the individual abilities of students. Most of these efforts have resulted in instruction that can be labeled *individualized instruction*. There are a number of ways to individualize instruction, such as allowing each student to proceed at his or her own pace, providing different instruc-

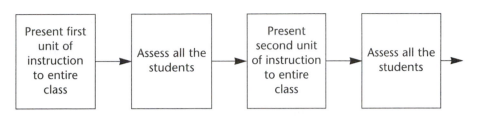

FIGURE 7-1
A Traditional Approach to Instruction

tional materials for different students, or allowing different students to work on different objectives. Almost all of these approaches result in serious classroom management problems. With so many students proceeding in so many different directions, it is almost impossible, even with the use of a computer, to keep track of individual students as they progress toward their individual instructional goals.

In addition to the management problems, many teachers who have taught in these situations note the strong desire of students to work together, whether it is in a small group or in a large group, under the direction of a teacher. Therefore, alternative approaches to total individualization have been proposed. One of the best known of these is the mastery learning approach proposed initially by Benjamin Bloom, an educator at the University of Chicago.

In this chapter, we will focus our attention on the mastery learning approach. We will do so because we believe it is an effective means of implementing instruction. While we realize that you may not use this approach to implement your instruction, we believe it is an approach you should be aware of and at least consider.

MAJOR CONCEPTS AND EXAMPLES

Those who advocate the mastery learning approach make several basic assumptions about students who are engaged in the learning process. They assume that the reason some students do not achieve under the present system is that their aptitude limits the speed at which they can acquire new information. However, they indicate that nearly all students can master given instructional objectives if they are given enough time to do so, if the instruction they receive is of reasonable quality, and if they are tested frequently in order to determine if they are achieving mastery. Thus, *mastery learning* advocates propose that the basic distinction between the mastery learning approach and typical group instruction involves the amount of time students are given to acquire a set of objectives and the extent to which they acquire those objectives. Under the group-instruction approach, all students are given the same amount of time and, as a result, performances vary among students. Conversely, under the mastery learning approach, the time available to acquire a set of objectives varies among students, and, consequently, most students eventually achieve about the same level of high performance.

How does the mastery learning approach operate? The sequence of instructional and assessment activities is depicted in Figure 7.2. As shown in the figure, as is the case with group instruction, the teacher presents a unit of instruction to the entire class (or group) and then assesses the group. However, rather than immediately moving on to the next unit, the teacher provides additional instruction to the students in light of how well they performed when they were assessed. Those students who learned, or *mastered,* the skills that were assessed receive some enrichment activities, while those who did not achieve mastery receive some form of remediation and are then reassessed. The time devoted to the enrichment, remedial, and retesting activities is up to the teacher but rarely exceeds a few classroom hours spread over two or three days. It is hoped (and often is found to be the case) that at this point most of the students who received

FIGURE 7-2
An Example of a Mastery Learning Approach

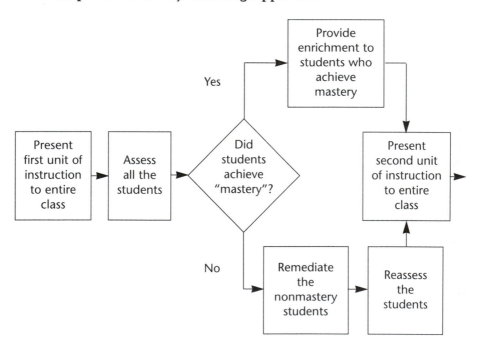

remediation have mastered the skills they were expected to acquire. The teacher then proceeds to presents the next unit of instruction to the entire class, and the same cycle of activities begins.

Planning for Mastery Learning

Let's examine what must occur before a mastery learning approach can be implemented in the classroom. First of all, there usually is a set of learning objectives that all students are expected to achieve and a set of test items that directly assess the behaviors described in the objectives.

Next comes a crucial step in planning for mastery learning—identifying the level of student performance that will constitute mastery. Those who have frequently used the mastery learning approach find that the best way to identify a mastery level of performance is to identify the level of performance of students who have received A's or B's in the past. Anything below that level is referred to as nonmastery. Therefore, a teacher might examine a twenty-item test, which has been designed to measure two objectives, and decide that a student must get at least eight out of ten items for each of the two objectives in order to achieve mastery. That decision might be based on the fact that previous students who had received an A or B in the course answered at least that many items correctly.

The next planning step is to combine sets of objectives into small units of instruction, each of which can be taught within a period of one or two weeks. By creating units of this size and assessing students at the end of each unit, you increase the likelihood that you will be able to identify and remediate student learning problems before they become practically insurmountable.

After you cluster your objectives into small units, you must decide upon the instructional activities that you will employ when the instruction is initially presented to your class as a whole. Then you must give considerable attention to the planning of individualized and/or small-group remedial and enrichment activities. If you are willing to engage in this level of preparation, you should be able to implement a mastery learning approach in your classroom.

It is interesting to note that if you have developed the plans called for in the application assignments in this book, you have many of the components required to implement a mastery learning strategy. You have the objectives, the assessment items, and the basic instructional approach. Perhaps the key element in the whole system is the remedial activities that follow the administration of a test. Research studies show that when mastery learning systems have failed, it has almost always been because of the failure of the teacher to follow up on the implementation of remedial strategies and on the reassessment of learners who initially failed to master a unit. Therefore, we can conclude that simply giving the formative examination and directing students to engage in remedial activities is not sufficient. We have to make sure that those remedial activities do, in fact, take place, that they are targeted on specific student deficiencies, and that we reexamine the students to certify that mastery has occurred. Without this step in the process, we will not be using the full capabilities of the mastery learning approach.

Sometimes it is difficult to determine what kinds of remedial activities will be effective for students who have not been able to master the objectives from the group instruction. Simply saying, "Go back and read the textbook again," has not proven very effective. What has proven effective is the use of peer tutors, older tutors, or small study-group sessions in which each student has an opportunity to teach and be taught. Obviously, when remedial activities such as these are used, the teacher must have confidence in his or her ability to control students under such conditions because it cannot be assumed that they will be highly motivated to participate in the remedial activities. To achieve this, it may be necessary to use various forms of rewards that are most appropriate for the students who are involved.

Results of Using the Mastery Learning Approach

Much research has been conducted in the last two decades on the use of the mastery learning strategy. In general, the results from that research indicate that typically two to three times as many students achieve mastery as previously achieved A's or B's in the course. That means that if in a traditionally taught course, 30 percent of the students are getting A's and B's, it would not be surprising to find that 60 percent to 90 percent of the students in a mastery learning course received A's and B's. It should be noted that these are perfectly legitimate, documented A's and B's that result from the alignment of objectives, tests, and instructional activities. The teacher is not giving out easy grades to students but grades that students earn by their performance in relation to prespecified standards.

Those who use mastery learning in their classrooms have also found that students tend to have more positive attitudes toward the skills that are learned in this fashion. The one exception to this finding has been in those situations in which the mastery learning standard has been set so high that students had to work beyond any reasonable level of expectation to achieve the mastery level. When this occurred, attitudes toward the content have suffered accordingly.

Research results also suggest, but offer little firm evidence, that students may learn "how to learn" more effectively under mastery learning systems. When a mastery learning approach is used, students learn that there are ways of learning in school other than simply listening to the teacher and reading the textbook. They learn that they can learn from other students and that they, in turn, can help other students to learn. They also become more aware of the importance of objectives and how these relate to the assessment of their own learning. Some mastery learning advocates contend that with this new knowledge in hand, students are better able to direct their own study activities, and thus they learn more and do so in less time.

One of the other effects of using the mastery learning approach is the tendency for teachers not only to examine the performance of their students, but also to examine their own performance. In other words, by examining the extent to which students are successful or unsuccessful in achieving mastery, teachers become very aware of the quality of the instruction they are providing. Furthermore, by examining the performance and attitudes of their students, mastery learning teachers usually become quickly aware of the need to revise their instruction.

Alternative Teaching Approaches

While we have provided a detailed description of a mastery learning approach, it is certainly not the only one that is available to the teacher. The authors of this book, as well as many of the readers, were successfully educated using what would be considered a traditional teaching approach. Such an approach differs primarily in terms of less frequent objectives-based testing and less concern for remediation of nonmasters. Others have learned from less formal learning situations in which students are encouraged, especially at the primary level, to explore both physical stimuli and abstract symbols in order to discover new knowledge. We will not try to argue which approach is best; each has its merits. At different times with different objectives, different approaches may be required.

Of great importance in planning the implementation of instruction is to consider the feasibility of any given approach. With regard to using the mastery learning approach, you must decide if you have the time and resources to use frequent testing and provide individualized and/or small-group enrichment and remediation activities to students. If you cannot do all of this, perhaps you can still adapt some aspects of the mastery learning approach when you implement instruction in your classroom.

In the problem scenario presented at the beginning of this chapter, Mr. Vallano was discouraged because so few of his students had performed well on the midterm examination he had administered. Perhaps if Mr. Vallano had employed some of the principles of mastery learning, especially the notion of frequent testing and individualized or small-group remediation, more of his students would have mastered the skills he wanted them to acquire.

PRACTICE

In this practice activity, we would like to have you consider the classroom setting in which you are likely to teach. Will it be possible to implement a mastery learning approach? We would not be surprised if your answer were "no" because so many factors must be present for the entire approach to be used successfully. However, it may be possible to use some of the components of a mastery learning approach. The major components are listed here. Indicate if you would or would not use each component, and why.

1. Provide students with objectives that indicate what they must learn to do.
2. Present initial instruction to all students at one time.
3. Provide frequent tests on objectives.
4. Provide students with appropriate remedial activities.
5. Provide students with sufficient time to master instruction.

FEEDBACK

There is no specific feedback for this practice activity. However, we hope you find your analysis of classroom instructional practices to be helpful as you prepare the application activity described below.

APPLICATION

Describe how the mastery learning approach could be used to implement the lesson plans and test you developed for the previous application assignments in this book.

SUMMARY

In this chapter, we have described an alternative to the traditional way in which instruction is implemented. This alternative, called the mastery learning approach, allows instructional time to vary among students so that most students can acquire (or "master") the skills we want them to attain.

Under the mastery learning approach, as is the case under traditional group instruction, the teacher presents a unit of instruction to the entire class and then assesses the group. However, rather than immediately moving on to the next unit, the teacher provides additional instruction to the students in light of how well they performed when they were assessed. Those students who learned, or *mastered,* the skills that were assessed, receive some enrichment activities, while those who did not achieve mastery receive some form of remediation and are then reassessed. Oftentimes, after students receive remediation, they are able to master the skills with which they had difficulty. The teacher then presents the next unit of instruction to the entire class, and the same cycle of activities begins.

Although it is likely that you will implement your instruction using a more traditional approach, there are several reasons why you should consider employing a mastery learning approach in your classroom. First, research has shown that the mastery learning approach has a positive effect on student attitude and student learning. And second, although much work is necessary to plan and implement a mastery learning approach, the plans you may have developed as you read through this book will provide you with many of the components required to implement a mastery learning strategy.

C H A P T E R 8

Revising Instruction

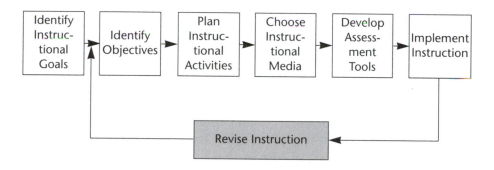

How many times have you attended classes in which it was apparent that the lesson being taught was the same one the teacher had been teaching for years? This situation would not be bad if the lesson were a good one, but oftentimes "old" lessons prove to be ineffective ones. The important point here is that lesson planning should not end when you first implement your lesson. Instead, if you gather information from students during implementation, you should be able to revise your instruction so that it will be more effective the next time it is presented.

PROBLEM SCENARIO

Ms. Hatten has just about come to the conclusion that it is impossible to teach high school students about the involvement of the United States in the Middle East. She has taught this topic for the past three years, and each year has had increasing difficulty in getting students to understand the importance of U.S. participation in Middle Eastern affairs. The students seem to understand a few of the basic concepts but then seem to get lost. Now Ms. Hatten is beginning to think that she should completely change her approach to this topic. How can she use data from students to identify the problems they are having and improve her instruction?

CHAPTER OBJECTIVES

The objectives for this chapter are that you will be able to:

1. describe the types of information that should be collected from students in order to improve instruction
2. interpret data that have been collected from students and indicate how instruction might be improved

BACKGROUND INFORMATION

Every teacher has had the experience of providing instruction that just did not work. Sometimes the problem with the instruction is obvious, but sometimes it is not. Our systematic view of instruction suggests that we must examine both the process of instruction, that is, what went on with the learners, as well as the results of the instruction, namely, the test performance and the attitudes of learners, in order to determine what went wrong and how it might be improved. It is important to note that this type of evaluation and revision is not focused on determining the value or worth of the instruction. It is a positive, constructive act that is considered a basic component of the teaching process, the purpose of which is to improve the instruction for future use.

When a lesson plan is prepared, many assumptions are made about such things as student skills, knowledge, and attitudes and the appropriateness of the content and instructional activities to be employed. These are determined by our experience and knowledge of the students and the instructional setting. When instruction is implemented, it provides an opportunity to see just how well the lesson was designed and, of equal importance, how it can be improved for use the next time. If there is no intention of ever offering the instruction again, then there is no need to be involved in these systematic review and revision processes. However, since most instruction is given on a repeated basis, it is critically important to revise lesson plans so that they become more and more effective. In this chapter, we will describe how test results and student attitude data can be used to improve the quality of your instructional activities.

MAJOR CONCEPTS AND EXAMPLES

In this section we will describe the data that can be collected from students, when it can be collected, and how it should be interpreted and used to revise instruction. Data should be collected concerning student performance and student attitudes. There is an interesting relationship between these two sets of information. The basic outcomes of instruction are almost always stated in terms of the performance of learners, and without that performance, attitudes are of little consequence. However, in your attempt to get students to perform well, you should not forget about their attitudes. Often teachers are equally concerned with the attitudes of learners as they are with their performance. Having a learning situation in which students perform successfully but do not have good feelings about the instruction is certainly not satisfactory to many teachers because students are unlikely to want to study the topic in the future. Therefore you should look at both performance and attitude.

What types of performance data should you collect? You should try to collect data that will tell you how well your students are able to perform your objectives as a result of the instruction they received. In order to gather this information, it is useful to assess students both before and after they participate in the lessons you have prepared for them. As you may know, the data collected prior to presenting these lessons is often referred to as pretest data, and that which you collect afterwards is often referred to as posttest data. Oftentimes it is too difficult and/or time-consuming to collect pretest information, but if you want to improve your instruction, posttest data should always be collected.

What means can you employ in order to gather pretest and posttest performance data? As we have previously indicated, paper-and-pencil tests are usually employed to gather data concerning student performance on intellectual skills and knowledge objectives. Observations using checklists or rating scales are often employed for motor skills and attitudinal outcomes.

It is also desirable to gather performance data during instruction. This can be done by collecting student performance data on practice exercises. It can also be done by administering several brief quizzes designed to assess student progress toward acquisition of the objectives that are being taught.

As for student attitudes, it is useful to gather data before, during, and after instruction. However, as with performance data, it may be too time-consuming to gather information about student attitudes prior to instruction on a particular topic. At the very least, however, you should try to gather student attitude data at the end of a sequence of instruction (be it a lesson, unit, or course).

Student attitude data can be gathered in a variety of ways. Questionnaires, interviews after the instruction, and observations of students during instruction are among the most common techniques for gathering attitude data. In each case, you should try to ascertain student attitudes toward specific instructional techniques you employed and specific topics that you covered. This information, rather than information about students' overall impressions, will help you identify specific strengths and weaknesses in your instruction.

Your own observation of student attitudes during instruction can also be a very useful data source. If, based upon student reactions in class, you feel that some activity went extremely well or extremely poorly, be sure to write a brief note to yourself regarding this matter. We have found this technique to be very helpful when, at a later date, we are attempting to revise a lesson we have previously taught. However, be careful when you use this technique; sometimes it is quite difficult to gauge accurately the reactions of students if you don't question them directly about this matter.

In summary, listed below are the types of information you should consider collecting. They are listed as essential and additional information; the latter depend on whether you have the time and resources to collect such data.

Essential Information

- student performance on posttests (look at performance on each objective separately)
- student attitudes following instruction

Additional Information

- student performance on pretests
- student attitudes prior to instruction
- student performance on practice exercises and quizzes during instruction
- observation of student attitudes during instruction

Steps in Analyzing Information

After all the data have been collected, organize and review them systematically to identify what went right and what went wrong. Although this may seem like a major task, it really is not.

Begin your analysis by scoring the test you gave at the end of the instruction for the objectives covered by your instructional plan. As you are scoring the test, be sure that you examine the incorrect responses that the students are making, perhaps even noting them on a separate piece of paper. This information is helpful to you in two ways. First, it may help you identify misconceptions the students have as a result of your instruction. Once you identify such misconceptions, you can revise your instruction so that the next time you teach, the students will be unlikely to make the same mistakes. For example, young students might say that the sun is closer to the earth than the moon is because the sun is brighter. This error could be dealt with directly the next time the lesson is taught.

Second, by noting the kinds of errors made by students, you should be able to detect defective test items—items that are not testing whether students have attained your objectives. How can you tell whether a test item is defective? For one, the nature of the incorrect responses often tell you whether students interpreted a question in the way in which you intended them to interpret it. Another indication is that a large number of the better students select the wrong answer. For the purposes of analyzing your instruction, student performance on defective items should be ignored, but the item should be revised if it is to be used again.

After you have scored the test and eliminated defective items, you should summarize the test data. This task can be made easier if you group your test items by the objectives they measure. By doing so, you can easily determine how well your students performed on each objective. This information can then be put on a chart that lists each student's name down the left side and each objective across the top. By looking down the columns of the chart, you will be able to quickly tell how well your class was able to perform on each objective.

In Table 8.1 you can see that eight students have taken a test that included items for four objectives. There were four items for each of the four objectives. You can use this table to identify those objectives students had difficulty with and to review your instructional activities for those objectives. For example, of the objectives listed in Table 8.1, there certainly appears to be a problem with Objective 4. For this objective it would be necessary to examine each component of the instructional plan to determine if it was appropriately planned and consistent with what we

TABLE 8.1:   Summary of Student Performance by Objective

Student	Objective Number				Average
	1	*2*	*3*	*4*	
Art	100	100	100	100	100
Bob	100	75	100	25	75
Claire	100	100	100	75	94
Donna	75	75	75	75	75
Ernest	50	0	50	0	25
Frank	100	75	100	50	81
Gloria	100	100	100	100	100
Helen	75	100	50	25	63
Average	88	78	84	56	77

know about the type of desired learning outcome. Often in this retro-spective phase, problems with instructional activities can be identified which were not apparent earlier.

At this point, you should also examine any pretest performance data that you gathered, as well as data regarding student performance on practice exercises and quizzes. Such data, when examined along with posttest data, may provide you with further insights. For example, your reaction to the posttest data for Objective 2 might be different if pretest data revealed that student performance on Objective 2 had not changed from pretest to posttest.

After student performance data have been analyzed, it is important to take into consideration the attitudes students express toward the instruction. First look at the attitude data you collected after your instruc-tional activities took place. Does this data indicate that students had a positive reaction to the instruction? If not, might poor performance on one or more objectives be related to negative student attitudes? If you measured student attitudes beforehand, did student attitudes prior to instruction differ from attitudes after the instruction was presented? At this point, it is also useful to examine the notes you took regarding stu-dent attitudes during instruction. These notes should not only remind you of the attitudes students exhibited during instruction, but should also give you clues as to which portions of your instruction might be in need of improvement, at least with regard to promoting positive student attitudes.

Revising Your Instructional Plans

When you examine the student performance and attitude data you col-lected, it is quite likely that you will identify weaknesses in your instruc-tion. How should you go about revising your instructional plans so as to correct these weaknesses? Let's examine the kinds of revisions that are often made at this point in the instructional process. First, as mentioned earlier, you may find that some of your test items must be revised because they do not measure the behaviors specified in your objectives. Howev-er, before you begin to revise your test items, it seems wise to review your objectives. Now that your instructional plan has been carried out and you have collected some data regarding its effectiveness, do you feel that your objectives can be achieved by your learners and that the objectives are appropriate for them? If the answer to both these questions is "yes," then you should proceed with further refinement of your test items and other components of your instructional plan. If, however, you find the answer is "no," then the first step is to reexamine each objective and either elim-inate it or rewrite it at a higher or lower level, depending upon the capa-bilities of your learners.

The rewriting of the objectives subsequently results in revisions to your test items and your instructional activities, but this extra work is necessary if you are interested in having an instructional plan that is appropriate for future use. For example, did the motivational aspects of your instruction really work? Did they attract and maintain the learners' interest during the lesson? What about the information and examples you provided to the learners? In retrospect, does it appear that there was sufficient instruction here, and were the examples adequate for all learners? In other words, there may be several activities in the plan that could be revised.

Practice and feedback are often the instructional activities that can make or break a lesson. These instructional events may simply consist of students responding to worksheets or may involve student participation in a complex simulation. Regardless of the complexity of the activity, it is during this event that students practice performing the behavior that they are required to attain and, we hope, receive feedback regarding that performance. Without adequate practice and feedback, students typically have difficulty acquiring the behavior. Thus, if this portion of the lesson is inadequate, for whatever reason, it is quite likely to be reflected by poor performance on the posttest. Therefore, the analysis of student performance on the practice and feedback portions of your strategy is important because it shows if students mastered the objectives at that point.

The effectiveness of practice and feedback activities can also be assessed in terms of student performance on any quizzes that you administer as part of your instructional plan. Sometimes we find that students do quite well on these quizzes but are unable to maintain that level of performance when they take a posttest. This seems to be particularly characteristic of below-average learners who can demonstrate immediate performance but have a great deal of difficulty retaining information for a long period of time. The situation calls for a strategy of frequent review of existing knowledge and frequent testing of that knowledge.

The final area of concern is that of remedial activities. If you use the mastery learning strategy, undoubtedly some of your students will need remedial work. These are the students who are least likely, in the absence of remedial work, to be able to demonstrate mastery of the objectives that are part of your instructional plan. Therefore, the quality of your remedial activities has a major bearing on the performance of these students.

If you carefully examine your remedial activities, you may be able to identify ineffective approaches that, if changed, will enable most of your students to acquire your objectives. For example, in our problem scenario, Ms. Hatten required students who failed her short-answer tests in the unit on United States involvement in the Middle East to read a three-page summary she wrote and then respond to a series of true or false questions. After engaging in this remedial activity, the students were given another short-answer test on the subject. Only three of the seventeen students who received the remedial materials were able to pass the second test. Obviously, the remedial activity Ms. Hatten has developed was not successful. Considering the nature of the test she gave, perhaps Ms. Hatten should not only improve the instruction she provided, but also require her students to respond to short-answer questions, rather than true or false items, during the remedial activity. In addition, she might consider interspersing test items throughout her summary sheets, rather than putting all the items at the end.

Revising Instruction: An Example

Let's look at another fictitious scenario to see how an instructional unit might be revised. Jean Chen, a middle school science teacher, has developed a unit that includes four objectives. The first three are knowledge objectives, one of which involves the recall of a formula; the fourth objective is an intellectual-skills objective that requires the students to use the formula to solve some problems.

Recently, Ms. Chen taught the unit for the first time. On Monday, she administered a pretest to the students and then gave them a lecture in which she presented the information related to the three knowledge objectives. On Tuesday, the class had a short discussion about the information that had been presented the previous day and then were given a quiz over that information. On Wednesday, the students were shown a film, which demonstrated a procedure for conducting a laboratory activity that involved the use of the formula the students had learned. After the film, the students who had passed the quiz were allowed to work on projects for the science fair while those students who failed were given a remedial information sheet to study and a worksheet to complete. On Thursday, Ms. Chen briefly reviewed the procedures that were to be used during the laboratory activity and then let the students conduct the exercise in the lab. On Friday, the students finished the lab activity and were given a posttest covering all four objectives for the unit. Ms. Chen then held a "debriefing session" with the class, during which time she elicited their opinions about the new unit.

After the unit was over, Ms. Chen examined the data she had collected. The pretest scores revealed that the students knew virtually nothing about the topic beforehand. The quiz results indicated that 80 percent of the students were able to master the first three objectives by Tuesday. The other students were able to answer all of the questions on the remediation worksheet and were subsequently able to master the first three objectives on Friday's posttest. However, the posttest data revealed that only 50 percent of the students in the class were able to master the fourth objective.

Ms. Chen also reviewed the notes she had taken during the unit. Her perceptions were that Monday's lecture and Tuesday's class discussion had gone quite well. The film and the remedial activity that were presented on Wednesday also seemed to be effective. However, the laboratory activity that took place on Thursday and Friday seemed to have some problems. The lab apparatus broke down several times and the worksheets the students were supposed to use contained a number of misprints. These conditions seemed to frustrate a number of the students.

Ms. Chen's perceptions were confirmed by the opinions the students expressed during the debriefing session on Friday. For the most part, the students' opinions about the unit were quite positive. However, they indicated that they were frustrated about the laboratory activity, primarily because of the problems with the apparatus and worksheets, but also because they thought the activity seemed unrelated to the unit; using the formula they had been taught was only a very small part of the activity.

Given this information, Ms. Chen tried to decide how to revise her instructional plan for the unit. First of all, she examined the test items and found that they accurately reflected her objectives. Then she reexamined the objectives and decided they were appropriate for her students. Ms. Chen then looked at her instructional activities. The students seemed motivated throughout the unit, with the exception of their frustration with the laboratory activity. Apparently the information she had presented to the students was adequate—most of the students were able to master the knowledge objectives without any difficulty. Even those students who initially failed to master these objectives were able to do so after the remedial activity; thus, the remedial activity also seemed to be a good one. However, whereas all of the students were able to recall the formula she had taught them, only half of them were able to apply it to solve the problems that appeared on the posttest. Ms. Chen decided that during the unit she would have to provide more examples of how the formula could be used.

Most of the problems with the unit seemed to center around the laboratory exercise. Ms. Chen examined those portions of her unit related to the laboratory exercise. She decided that although the film seemed to describe clearly how to conduct the laboratory activity, the problems with the lab apparatus and worksheets obviously contributed to the students' sense of frustration. These problems would have to be resolved if the laboratory activity was conducted again. However, the students' comments about the lack of relevance of the laboratory activity led Ms. Chen to reexamine its appropriateness in relation to her objectives. In doing so, she decided that the next time she taught the unit she would change the laboratory exercise to focus more directly on the formula she wanted her students to be able to use. As a result of this decision, she also had to find a replacement for the film she had used, as well as develop a different worksheet for the new laboratory activity. The lab apparatus her students would use for this activity would also be somewhat different from the apparatus that had been used the first time.

By examining the data she had collected, Ms. Chen decided to change her instructional plan for the unit in several fairly significant ways. Her objectives and tests would remain the same, as would her remedial activity and the first two days of her instructional activities. However, the film and laboratory exercises would be replaced. Furthermore, her revised plan would call for her to spend more time providing the students with examples of how to use the formula they had memorized. Although these changes were rather substantial, Ms. Chen was eager to make them, feeling that they would result in making her instruction more effective.

PRACTICE

1. Assume that you are responsible for teaching a high school career education class. There are twenty-two students in the class. One of the major objectives of the class is that the students will be able to complete an application form for a job successfully. You prepare and implement an instructional plan for the objective. Describe the various types of data and information you would collect in order to evaluate and revise the instructional plan.
2. Mr. Lyons, a physical education major, has been hired as a new teacher at a local elementary school. His first assignment is to teach a unit of physical fitness. It seems that the unit was taught last year to some fourth graders and data have been collected. Mr. Lyons' responsibility is to examine how the unit was taught and revise the methodology before teaching it next week.

   Mr. Lyons finds that there are three major objectives related to the physical fitness goal: (a) students will be able to do five consecutive push-ups, (b) students will be able to do two consecutive chin-ups, and (c) students will be able to run a quarter mile in four minutes.

   The plan used by the instructor who previously taught the unit indicated that he motivated the students by telling them how important it is to be physically fit. Subsequently, he showed the students how to do push-ups and chin-ups, and simply told them they would have to be able to run around the track in four minutes or less. After this instruction, the students were organized into groups and spent the next several days practicing each of the three objectives. At the end of the week, each student was individually tested on the three objectives. The results were as follows:

   A. five push-ups: 80 percent of the students were successful
   B. two chin-ups: 30 percent of the students were successful
   C. run a quarter mile in four minutes: 50 percent of the students were successful.

   When Mr. Lyons talked with the students about the instruction, there were a great variety of reactions, ranging from those who were very enthusiastic to those who thought it was extremely poor. Mr. Lyons now must decide what to do with all of this information.

Based on the scenario, answer the following questions:

A. How would you examine the data and information the previous teacher provided for Mr. Lyons?
B. What do the data tell you about the effectiveness of the previous teacher's instructional plan?
C. If you were Mr. Lyons, how would you change the instructional plan before you taught the unit?

FEEDBACK

For the two practice activities in this chapter, your answers may be somewhat different from ours, but should cover many of the same points.

1. Below is a description of the types of data and information we would collect if we were evaluating an instructional plan designed to teach students how to complete a job application successfully. First, on the day we began teaching this topic, we would try to ascertain the basic reading and writing competencies of the students and the extent to which they were already able to fill out a job application form from a local company.

   Second, during the instruction we would have a practice activity which would involve having the students fill out a job application form. When we evaluated our instructional plan, we would want to know how well the students were able to fill out this form. The information we gather should give us a good indication of the effectiveness of the instruction delivered prior to practice exercises.

   Third, we would administer a posttest that was similar to the pretest. In other words, on the posttest, the students would again be required to fill out a job application form. This form would not be the same one that was used on the pretest, nor would it be the same as the form used during the practice exercise. Student performance on this test would give us a good indication of the success of our instructional strategy, including the practice, feedback, and remedial activities.

   Fourth, at the end of the unit, we would ask the students to respond to a very brief questionnaire in which we would ask them about any problems they had with the instruction and the posttest. We would also ask them about their attitudes toward the instruction. Fifth, we would take notes concerning our delivery of the instruction as well as our perceptions regarding student responses to the instruction.

By collecting all of these types of data, we should be able to evaluate the effectiveness of our instruction, as well as identify those sections of the instructional plan that should be revised.

2. Listed below is a description of how Mr. Lyons went about examining and interpreting the data the previous teacher provided for him and how he changed the instructional plan for the unit. It just so happens that Mr. Lyons, having recently read this book, performed each of these tasks in an exemplary manner! Therefore, we hope that your response is similar to what is described below.

   The first thing Mr. Lyons did was examine whether the assessment activities the previous teacher employed measured the behaviors described in the objectives for the unit. Having found that they did, he checked the literature from the President's Council on Physical Fitness to make sure that the objectives were appropriate for the students, and he determined that they were. Next, Mr. Lyons reviewed the data that were collected when the previous teacher assessed the students at the end of the unit. Since at the end of the unit only 30 percent of the students were able to do two chin-ups and only 50 percent of the students were able to run a quarter mile in four minutes, the unit was judged not to be very effective. Furthermore, Mr. Lyons was not particularly impressed by the fact that by the end of the lesson, 80 percent of the students were able to do five push-ups. He reasoned that since the students were not pretested, it was impossible to tell whether the students might have been able to perform this feat before instruction. If most of them were already able to do 5 push-ups, then the unit was quite unsuccessful.

   When Mr. Lyons reviewed the comments the students made regarding the unit, he concluded that perhaps the wide range of opinions expressed by the students reflected their general attitudes toward physical fitness and that the instructional unit had little, if any, effect on those attitudes.

   Having analyzed the data the previous teacher provided for him, and having decided that the unit had very little effect on student performance and attitudes, Mr. Lyons decided that he would make some extensive revisions in the instructional plan before he taught the unit. Since the objectives and assessment activities for the unit seemed appropriate, Mr. Lyons decided that other than adding a pretest, he would not change these. However, when he reviewed the various activities that comprised the instructional plan for the unit, he decided that a number of major changes were in order.

   First, he concluded that although the three objectives for the unit involved motor skills, the chances that the children would acquire those skills would be greatly increased if they had positive attitudes about being physically fit. He felt the children were unlikely to acquire a positive attitude simply by having their instructor tell them how important it was to be fit. Therefore, he decided to begin the unit with a film in which a role model for the children demonstrated the motor skills and briefly discussed the benefits of being physically fit. In addition, Mr. Lyons decided that when he taught the children how to perform these skills, he would have them demonstrated by children who passed the pretest or by respected children from the next higher grade. He decided to do this because he felt that the students would be encouraged to perform the skills if they saw them performed by other children they admired.

Mr. Lyons also decided that during the days that the students would be practicing the skills, he would set up three "check-out stations" to assess individual student progress toward attainment of the three objectives. At first, he and the students who passed the pretest would be the evaluators at the three stations. As more students demonstrated mastery of the objectives, they would be asked to help at the stations and assist some of the other students. Thus, Mr. Lyons would have more time to work with those students who were having the most difficulty. He felt that by using these procedures while the students were practicing the skills, he would greatly increase the chances that a much larger percentage of the students would acquire the skills by the end of the unit and, hopefully, would have better attitudes toward physical fitness.

APPLICATION

Describe the plan you will use for collecting data and information to revise the lesson plans you developed. Indicate what data and information you will collect, when you will collect it, and how you will collect it. Also indicate how that information will be used to identify problems and subsequently to revise your lesson plans.

SUMMARY

In this chapter, we have encouraged you to prepare for the possibility that your lesson plans will not work perfectly the first time. In order to revise them, we suggested that basic information on student performance and attitudes should be collected prior to, during, and after the implementation of instruction.

After the instruction, the data for each of your objectives should be summarized. In doing so, you should verify that your test items accurately assessed the behaviors specified in your objectives and that your objectives were appropriate ones. In those cases where many students failed to attain an objective, a review of the various components of your instructional plan for that objective is necessary. You must determine what revisions are needed before the next implementation of your lesson plans.

C H A P T E R   9

Summary and Concluding Thoughts

As we indicated at the outset of this book, instructional planning is one of the most important activities teachers engage in. As a teacher, you will make decisions when you plan your instruction that not only will affect what you do in your classroom, but also will have a significant influence on what your students learn and their attitudes toward what is being taught.

KEY PRINCIPLES UNDERLYING THE SYSTEMATIC PLANNING PROCESS

In this book we have described a seven-step systematic approach to instructional planning. There are four key principles underlying this systematic planning process. Each of these principles is described below.

The first principle is that you should begin the planning process by clearly describing the general goals and specific objectives you want your students to attain. This approach to instructional planning is often referred to as an "objectives-first" approach. We believe in an objectives-first approach because if you don't have a clear picture of where you want your students to go, you will have a difficult time planning how to get them there! We also believe that an important part of this step in the planning process involves identifying the type of learning outcome each of your objectives represent. These types, or domains, of learning outcomes include knowledge, intellectual skills, motor skills, and attitudes.

The second key planning principle is that your instructional activities should be designed so as to help students attain your objectives. We have described six types of instructional activities that should normally be included in a lesson and have indicated that certain subsets of these activities should be given particular emphasis depending upon the type of learning outcome you would like your students to attain.

The third key principle underlying our systematic planning process is that your assessment tools should be designed to measure student attainment of your objectives. Appropriate assessment tools will provide students with an indication of their progress in mastering objectives and will provide you with information regarding the effectiveness of your instruction. This leads us to the next key principle.

The fourth key principle is that you should revise your instruction in light of the student performance on each objective and student attitude toward the instructional activities in which they participated. In order to make such revisions, it is important that the data you collect be directly related to specific objectives. Moreover, it is useful to collect such data before and during the instructional process, as well as after it.

THE ADAPTABILITY OF THE PROCESS

Will you and other teachers use the systematic planning process described in this book? In a variety of instructional settings, systematic planning processes like the one we have described have been adopted and have proven to be very effective. For example, many training organizations in large corporations, school systems in developing countries, and military organizations in the United States have successfully employed such planning procedures. However, research examining the planning practices of teachers in schools in the United States has indicated that although many teachers have been taught how to use some sort of systematic approach to instructional planning, few of them use such an approach after they enter the "real world" of teaching. Why is this the case? Some teachers have indicated that such approaches are too time-consuming and rigid.

In the seven years since we wrote the first edition of this book, we have spent considerable time examining the instructional planning practices of teachers. In this edition, we have tried to propose a planning process that reflects the basic principles underlying systematic instructional planning but also can be adapted to accommodate many of the planning practices most teachers have traditionally employed. Usually this has resulted in our pointing to a simpler way of carrying out some portion of the systematic planning process or has resulted in a suggestion that is more in keeping with the planning practices most teachers are accustomed to. For example, we have indicated that:

- As you gain experience using the approach we have described, it is likely that your written plans will become much sketchier; much of what you now are putting in writing will be done mentally.

Indeed, as an example, in Chapter 4 we presented an example of the same plan written at three different levels of detail, from very detailed to quite sketchy.

- It is often appropriate to write shortened versions of objectives, leaving out one or more of the the three basic components.
- In many cases, you will not need to be concerned about writing objectives at all; they will be provided to you via curriculum guides, teachers guides, textbooks, and other planning documents.
- When you are planning your instructional activities, it may be useful to employ an "objectives-second" approach (in which you first plan your activities and then identify the objectives those activities support).

These examples illustrate that the systematic planning process we have described is a flexible procedure that can be adapted in light of your previous teaching experiences and the instructional situation you are facing. As we indicated at the beginning of this book, a similar point of view has been expressed by two researchers (Clark and Peterson, 1986) who conducted perhaps the most thorough review of teacher planning practices. These researchers indicate that "it may be that training novice teachers in the use of a version of the rational [i.e., systematic] planning model provides them with an appropriate foundation for developing a planning style compatible with their own personal characteristics and with the task environment in which they must teach."

As you might guess, we strongly agree with the point of view expressed in the previous quotation! We believe that the planning process we have described in this book will provide you with a firm understanding of some of the key elements to consider as you go about planning instruction. But we also recognize the fact that as you gain teaching experience, it is quite likely that your approach to planning will deviate from the process we have described. Nonetheless, we hope that by having been exposed to this process and by having had the opportunity to practice using it in the manner we prescribe, you will be more likely to continue to employ the key principles that are part of the process. If you do so, we firmly believe you will be a more effective teacher.

Glossary

Note: We have attempted to define the terms listed in this glossary in accordance with the way the terms were used in this book. Many of the terms have other meanings in other contexts.

ATTITUDE.   A type (or domain) of learning outcome that focuses upon the personal choices of students. These choices are based upon students' feelings and beliefs.

AUTHENTIC ASSESSMENT.   Assessment that requires the student to perform a skill in the context in which the skill would be used outside the classroom.

BEHAVIOR.   That component of an objective which describes what the students will be expected to do, that is, the observable action they will be expected to take, as a result of instruction.

CHECKLIST.   A set of criteria used for judging the adequacy of a students' performance. The criteria often consist of descriptions of the characteristics of a successful performance. Checklists are usually used to assess students' attainment of motor skills or to evaluate student products.

CONCEPT.   A label used to describe a group of related things or ideas. Examples of concepts include "chair," "dictatorship," "planet," and "red".

CONCEPT LEARNING.   A type of learning outcome (within the intellectual skills domain) that focuses on the ability to identify whether specific things or ideas can be classified as examples of a particular concept.

CONDITIONS.   That component of an objective which describes the tools and circumstances under which a student will be expected to perform a desired behavior.

CRITERION.   That component of an objective which describes how well (and perhaps, how quickly) a student will be expected to perform a desired behavior.

CRITERION-REFERENCED TEST.   *See* Objective-Referenced Test.

DRILL-AND-PRACTICE PROGRAM.   An instructional program, presented by a computer, designed to provide students with the opportunity to practice skills or to rehearse knowledge previously presented to them.

EFFECTIVE INSTRUCTION.   Instruction that enables students to acquire specified skills, knowledge, and attitudes, and which students enjoy.

ENRICHMENT.   Instructional activities intended to extend student knowledge or skills beyond that which is required.

EXAMPLES.   Instances depicting the proper performance of a given behavior.

EXECUTIVE ROUTINE.   The series of steps that must be followed in the process of performing a motor skill.

FEEDBACK.   The information a student receives regarding the answer or answers he or she provided. At a minimum, feedback lets the student know whether the answer was correct. In addition, feedback may indicate what the correct answer was, why it was correct, and, perhaps, what was wrong with the student's incorrect answer.

FORMATIVE EXAMINATION.   A type of test, used as a component of the mastery learning approach, designed to assess student progress toward attainment of a given set of objectives.

GOALS.   Statements of desired outcomes of instruction, usually described in general terms. Goals may focus on outcomes related to schools, teachers, or students.

GROUP INSTRUCTION.   The process by which all the students in a class participate in the same instructional activities at the same time.

INDIVIDUALIZED INSTRUCTION.   Instruction tailored to the individual abilities of students. Means of individualizing instruction include allowing each student to proceed through instruction at his or her own pace, providing different instructional materials for different students, and allowing different students to work on different objectives.

INFORMATION.   The content (substance) a student needs to know in order to be able to attain a given objective.

INSTRUCTIONAL ACTIVITIES.   The steps (events) that take place when instruction is presented to students.

INSTRUCTIONAL DESIGN.   A systematic process for designing, developing, implementing, and evaluating instruction.

INSTRUCTIONAL GAME.   An instructional program, sometimes presented by a computer, designed to have students practice performing a particular skill in the context of a game.

INSTRUCTIONAL PLAN.   A brief description of the goals, objectives, test items, and instructional activities for a given segment of instruction.

INTELLECTUAL SKILL.   A type (or domain) of learning outcome that focuses on the ability to use, rather than state simply, information. Types of intellectual skills include concept learning, rule using, and problem solving.

KNOWLEDGE.   A type (or domain) of learning outcome that focuses on the ability to recall and state specific information.

LEARNING OUTCOMES.   Description of what students should be able to do as a result of instruction. This term may either refer to objectives or to goals that focus upon student behaviors.

MASTERY.   A level of performance (with respect to a particular objective or set of objectives) considered to be satisfactory or better.

MASTERY LEARNING APPROACH.   An instructional approach in which the instructional time spent on a set of objectives varies among students so that most students eventually attain all of the objectives. Underlying the mastery learning approach is the theory that nearly all students can master a given set of instructional objectives if they are allowed enough time to do so, if the instruction they receive is of a reasonable quality, and if they are tested frequently in order to determine whether they are achieving mastery.

MEDIA.   The physical means by which instruction is delivered to students.

MEDIA HARDWARE.   The equipment, such as computers, televisions, and tape players, that is used to present mediated materials (media software).

MEDIA SOFTWARE.   The instructional materials that are presented using a piece of media hardware.

MEDIATED MATERIALS.   *See* Media Software.

MOTOR SKILL.   A type (or domain) of learning outcome that focuses upon the ability to perform physical movement(s).

OBJECTIVE-REFERENCED TEST.   A test designed to measure student ability to perform the behaviors specified in a given set of objectives. This type of test is also known as a criterion-referenced test.

OBJECTIVES.   Explicit statements of what students will be able to do at the end of a segment of instruction.

PRACTICE.   The opportunity students are given to perform a particular behavior prior to the time when they are tested. Feedback usually accompanies practice.

PREREQUISITE SKILLS.   The skills, knowledge, and attitudes students must possess in order to be ready for (capable of understanding) instruction on related skills, knowledge, or attitudes.

PROBLEM SOLVING.   A type of learning outcome (within the intellectual skills domain) that focuses upon the ability to choose, as well as use, the rules needed to solve a particular problem. For example, a student who solves a word problem in mathematics without being told what rules to use in order to solve the problem is said to have engaged in problem solving.

REMEDIATION.   Instructional activities designed to enable students to attain an objective that they were unable to attain previously.

RULE.   A description of a means of arriving at a solution to a particular type of problem. Rules usually are composed of a combination of concepts. An example of a rule would be "when adding two fractions with the same denominator, add the two numerators and place them over the common denominator."

RULE USING.   A type of learning outcome (within the intellectual skills domain) that focuses upon the ability to use a given rule to solve a particular type of problem.

SIMULATION.   An instructional program, usually presented by a computer, designed to provide students with a simplified model of some aspect of the real world and give the student the opportunity to interact with that model in a real-life manner.

SKILL-ALIGNMENT CHECK.   The process of determining whether there is congruence between instructional objectives, instructional content, and tests. In other words, the process of determining whether the skills specified in a given set of objectives are the same skills as those being taught and those being tested.

SKILLS TRACE.   *See* Skill-Alignment Check.

STANDARD.   *See* Criterion.

TUTORIAL PROGRAM.   An instructional program, usually presented by a computer, designed to provide students with instructional information and examples related to a given objective. The program may also provide students with the opportunity to practice the behavior specified in the objective.

VALIDITY.   A test item or test is considered to be valid (to possess validity) if it measures the behavior (that is, knowledge, skill, or attitude) it was intended to measure.

Bibliography

Instructional Planning: Systematic Approaches

Dick, W., & Carey, L. M. (1996). *The systematic design of instruction.* (4th ed.). New York: HarperCollins.

Gagne, R. M., Briggs, L. J., & Wager, W. (1992). *Principles of instructional design.* (4th ed.). New York: Holt, Rinehart and Winston.

Kemp, J. E., Morrison, G. R., & Ross, S. M. (1994). *Designing effective instruction.* New York: Merrill.

Smith P. L., & Ragan, T. J. (1993). *Instructional design.* New York: Macmillan.

Sullivan, H., & Higgins, N. (1983). *Teaching for competence.* New York: Teachers College Press.

Instructional Planning: Research

Clark, C., & Dunn, S. (1991). Second generation research on teacher planning. In H. C. Waxman & H. J. Walberg (Eds.), *Effective teaching: Current research* Berkeley, CA: McCuthan, 183–201.

Clark, C., & Peterson, P. (1986). Teacher's thought process. In M. C. Wittrock (Ed.), *Handbook of research on teaching.* New York: Macmillan, 255–296.

McCutcheon, G. (1980). How do elementary school teachers plan? The nature of planning and influences on it. *The Elementary School Journal, 81,* 4–23.

Reiser, R. A. (1994). Examining the planning practices of teachers: Reflections on three years of research. *Educational Technology, 34*(3), 11–16.

Shavelson, R. (1983). Review of research on teachers' pedagogical judgments, plans, and decisions. *The Elementary School Journal, 83,* 392–413.

Instructional Planning: Success Stories

Bowsher, J. E. (1989). *Educating America: Lessons learned in the nation's corporations.* New York: Wiley.

Morgan, R. M. (1989). Instructional systems development in third world countries. *Educational Technology Research & Development, 37,* 47–56.

Assessment

Carey, L. M. (1994). *Measuring and evaluating school learning.* (2d. ed.). Boston: Allyn and Bacon.

Oosterhof, A. (1994). *Classroom applications of educational measurement.* (2d. ed.). New York: Merrill.

Mastery Learning

Block, J. H., Efthim, H. E., & Burns, R. B. (1989). *Building effective mastery learning schools.* New York: Longman.

Bloom, B. S. (1976). *Human characteristics and school learning.* New York: McGraw-Hill.

Bloom, B. S. (1981). *All our children learning.* New York: McGraw-Hill.

Media

Alessi, S. M., & Trollip, S. R. (1985). *Computer-based instruction: Methods and development.* Englewood Cliffs, NJ: Prentice-Hall.

Hannafin, M. J., & Peck, K. C. (1988). *The design, development and evaluation of instructional software.* (New York: Macmillan).

Reiser, R. A. & Gagne, R. M. (1983). *Selecting media for instruction.* Englewood Cliffs, NJ: Educational Technology Publications.

Objectives

Bloom, B. S. (1956). *Taxonomy of educational objectives: Cognitive domain.* New York: David McKay.

Mager, R. F. (1984). *Preparing instructional objectives.* (Rev. 2d ed.). Belmont, CA: Pitman Learning.

Theories of Learning Related to Systematic Planning

Gagne, R. M. (1985). *The conditions of learning.* (4th ed.). New York: Holt, Rinehart and Winston.

Gagne, R. M., & Driscoll, M. P. (1988). *Essentials of learning for instruction.* (2d ed.) Englewood Cliffs, NJ: Prentice-Hall.

Martin, B. L., & Briggs, L. J. (1986). *The affective and cognitive domains: Integration for instruction and research.* Englewood Cliffs, NJ: Educational Technology Publications.

Index